FORWARD/COMMENTARY

The National Institute of Standards and Technology (NIST) is a measurement standards laboratory, and a non-regulatory agency of the **United States Department of Commerce**. Its mission is to promote innovation and industrial competitiveness. Founded in 1901, as the National Bureau of Standards, NIST was formed with the mandate to provide standard weights and measures, and to serve as the national physical laboratory for the United States. **With a** world-class measurement and testing laboratory encompassing a wide range of areas of computer science, mathematics, statistics, and systems engineering, NIST's cybersecurity program supports its overall mission to promote U.S. innovation and industrial competitiveness by advancing measurement science, standards, and related technology through research and development in ways that enhance economic security and improve our quality of life.

The need for cybersecurity standards and best practices that address interoperability, usability and privacy has been shown to be critical for the nation. NIST's cybersecurity programs seek to enable greater development and application of practical, innovative security technologies and methodologies that enhance the country's ability to address current and future computer and information security challenges.

The cybersecurity publications produced by NIST cover a wide range of cybersecurity concepts that are carefully designed to work together to produce a holistic approach to cybersecurity primarily for government agencies and constitute the best practices used by industry. This holistic strategy to cybersecurity covers the gamut of security subjects from development of secure encryption standards for communication and storage of information while at rest to how best to recover from a cyber-attack.

Why buy a book you can download for free?   We print this so you don't have to.

Some are available only in electronic media. Some online docs are missing pages or barely legible.

We at 4th Watch Publishing are former government employees, so we know how government employees actually use the standards. When a new standard is released, an engineer prints it out, punches holes and puts it in a 3-ring binder. While this is not a big deal for a 5 or 10-page document, many NIST documents are over 100 pages and printing a large document is a time-consuming effort. So, an engineer that's paid $75 an hour is spending hours simply printing out the tools needed to do the job. That's time that could be better spent doing engineering. We publish these documents so engineers can focus on what they were hired to do – engineering. It's much more cost-effective to just order the latest version from Amazon.com

If there is a standard you would like published, let us know. Our web site is www.usgovpub.com

Many of our titles are available as ePubs for Kindle, iPad, Nook, remarkable, BOOX, and Sony eReaders.

Why buy an eBook when you can access data on a website for free? HYPERLINKS

Yes, many books are available as a PDF, but not all PDFs are bookmarked? Do you really want to search a 6,500-page PDF document manually? Load our copy onto your Kindle, PC, iPad, Android Tablet, Nook, or iPhone (download the FREE kindle App from the APP Store) and you have an easily searchable copy. Most devices will allow you to easily navigate an ePub to any Chapter. Note that there is a distinction between a Table of Contents and "Page Navigation". Page Navigation refers to a different sort of Table of Contents. Not one appearing as a page in the book, but one that shows up on the device itself when the reader accesses the navigation feature. Readers can click on a navigation link to jump to a Chapter or Subchapter. Once there, most devices allow you to "pinch and zoom" in or out to easily read the text. (Unfortunately, downloading the free sample file at Amazon.com does not include this feature. You have to buy a copy to get that functionality, but as inexpensive as eBooks are, it's worth it.) Kindle allows you to do word search and Page Flip (temporary place holder takes you back when you want to go back and check something). Visit **www.usgovpub.com** to learn more.

DRAFT

NIST SPECIAL PUBLICATION 1800-19A

Trusted Cloud

Security Practice Guide for VMware Hybrid Cloud Infrastructure as a Service (IaaS) Environments

Volume A:
Executive Summary

Donna Dodson
NIST

Daniel Carroll
Dell/EMC

Gina Scinta
Gemalto

Hemma Prafullchandra
HyTrust

Harmeet Singh
IBM

Raghuram Yeluri
Intel

Tim Shea
RSA

Carlos Phoenix
VMware

August 2018

PRELIMINARY DRAFT 1

This publication is available free of charge from: https://www.nccoe.nist.gov/projects/building-blocks/trusted-cloud/hybrid

Executive Summary

1   ▪   Cloud services can provide organizations the opportunity to increase their flexibility, availability,
2   resiliency, and scalability, which they can use in turn to increase security, privacy, efficiency,
3   responsiveness, innovation, and competitiveness.

4   ▪   The core impediments to an organization's broader adoption of cloud technologies are the
5   ability to protect its information and virtual assets in the cloud, and to have sufficient visibility
6   so it can conduct oversight and ensure that it (and its cloud provider) are complying with
7   applicable laws and business practices.

8   ▪   The National Cybersecurity Center of Excellence (NCCoE) at NIST built a laboratory environment
9   using commercial off-the-shelf technology and cloud services to safeguard the security and
10   privacy of an organization's applications and data being run within or transferred between
11   private and hybrid/public clouds.

12   ▪   The full NIST Cybersecurity Practice Guide being developed for this project will demonstrate
13   how organizations can implement trusted compute pools in order to enforce and monitor their
14   security and privacy policies on their cloud workloads and meet compliance requirements as
15   specified in NIST Special Publication 800-53 and the Cybersecurity Framework.

16 ## CHALLENGE

17 In cloud environments, workloads are constantly being spun up, scaled out, moved around, and shut
18 down. Organizations often find adopting cloud technologies is not a good business proposition because
19 they encounter one or more of the following issues:

20   1.   Cannot maintain consistent security and privacy protections for information—applications, data,
21   and related metadata—across platforms, even for a single class of information.

22   2.   Do not have the flexibility to be able to dictate how different information is protected, such as
23   providing stronger protection for more sensitive information.

24   3.   Cannot retain visibility into how their information is protected to ensure consistent compliance
25   with legal and business requirements.

26 Many organizations, especially those in regulated sectors like finance and healthcare, face additional
27 challenges because security and privacy laws vary around the world. For protecting information the
28 organization collects, processes, transmits, or stores, laws may vary depending on whose information it
29 is, what kind of information it is, and where it is located. Cloud technologies may silently move an
30 organization's data from one jurisdiction to another. Because laws in some jurisdictions may conflict
31 with an organization's own policies or local laws and regulations, an organization may decide it needs to
32 restrict which on-premises private or hybrid/public cloud servers it uses based on their geolocations to
33 avoid compliance issues.

34 ## SOLUTION

35 Organizations need to be able to monitor, track, apply, and enforce their security and privacy policies on
36 their cloud workloads based on business requirements in a consistent, repeatable, and automated way.
37 A cloud workload is an abstraction of the actual instance of a functional application that is virtualized or

38 containerized to include compute, storage, and network resources. Building on previous NIST work
39 documented in NIST Interagency Report (IR) 7904, *Trusted Geolocation in the Cloud: Proof of Concept*
40 *Implementation*, the NCCoE is developing a Trusted Cloud solution that will demonstrate how trusted
41 compute pools leveraging hardware roots of trust can provide the necessary security capabilities. These
42 capabilities will not only provide assurance that cloud workloads are running on trusted hardware and in
43 a trusted geolocation or logical boundary, but also will improve the protections for the data in the
44 workloads and data flows between workloads.

45 The example solution will leverage modern commercial off-the-shelf technology and cloud services to
46 address a particular use case scenario: lifting and shifting a typical multi-tier application between an
47 organization-controlled private cloud to a hybrid/public cloud over the Internet. The example solution
48 will include the following capabilities:

49 ▪ Data protection and encryption key management enforcement focused on trust-based and
50 geolocation-based/resource pools, and secure migration of cloud workloads.

51 ▪ Key management and keystore controlled by the organization, not the cloud service provider.

52 ▪ Persistent data flow segmentation before and after the trust-based and geolocation-
53 based/resource pools secure migration.

54 ▪ Industry sector and/or organizational business compliance enforcement for regulated workloads
55 between the on-premises private and hybrid/public clouds.

56 While the NCCoE will use a suite of commercial products to address this challenge, the practice guide
57 will not endorse these particular products, nor will it guarantee compliance with any regulatory
58 initiatives. Your organization's information security experts should identify the products that will best
59 integrate with your existing tools and IT system infrastructure. Your organization can adopt this solution
60 or one that adheres to these guidelines in whole, or you can use this guide as a starting point for
61 tailoring and implementing parts of a solution.

BENEFITS

63 Once available, the NCCoE's full practice guide to Trusted Cloud can help your organization:

64 ▪ Understand how trusted cloud technologies can reduce risk and satisfy existing system security
65 and privacy requirements.

66 ▪ Become aware of the resources, skills, experience, and knowledge needed to implement and
67 manage a trusted cloud environment.

68 ▪ Provide a practical and effective way to design and implement trusted cloud technologies,
69 including restricting cloud workloads to on-premises private or hybrid/public cloud servers
70 meeting specific characteristics.

71 ▪ Gain the ability to determine each cloud workload's security posture at any time through
72 continuous monitoring, regardless of the cloud infrastructure or server.

73 ▪ Modernize the legacy on-premises infrastructure by lifting and shifting existing workloads to the
74 cloud environment while maintaining control and visibility of the workloads.

75 ▪ Foster greater confidence in adoption of cloud technologies.

SHARE YOUR FEEDBACK

The comment period for the preliminary draft of this volume ends September 30, 2018. Comments may be submitted to trusted-cloud-nccoe@nist.gov with the Subject "Comments on Trusted Hybrid Cloud VolA-PD1." All comments are subject to release under the Freedom of Information Act (FOIA). There will be at least one additional comment period for this volume.

The other volumes of this guide will be released for review and comment on different schedules so that each volume is made available as soon as possible, rather than delaying the release of completed volumes until all other volumes are also completed. You will be able to view or download them at https://www.nccoe.nist.gov/projects/building-blocks/trusted-cloud/hybrid. Help the NCCoE make this guide better by sharing your thoughts with us as you read the guide. If you adopt this solution for your own organization, please share your experience and advice with us. We recognize that technical solutions alone will not fully enable the benefits of our solution, so we encourage organizations to share lessons learned and best practices for transforming the processes associated with implementing this guide.

TECHNOLOGY PARTNERS/COLLABORATORS

Organizations participating in this project submitted their capabilities in response to an open call in the Federal Register for all sources of relevant security capabilities from academia and industry (vendors and integrators). The following respondents with relevant capabilities or product components (identified as "Technology Partners/Collaborators" herein) signed a Cooperative Research and Development Agreement to collaborate with NIST in a consortium to build this example solution.

Certain commercial entities, equipment, products, or materials may be identified by name or company logo or other insignia in order to acknowledge their participation in this collaboration or to describe an experimental procedure or concept adequately. Such identification is not intended to imply special status or relationship with NIST or recommendation or endorsement by NIST or NCCoE; neither is it intended to imply that the entities, equipment, products, or materials are necessarily the best available for the purpose.

The National Cybersecurity Center of Excellence (NCCoE), a part of the National Institute of Standards and Technology (NIST), is a collaborative hub where industry organizations, government agencies, and academic institutions work together to address businesses' most pressing cybersecurity challenges. Through this collaboration, the NCCoE develops modular, easily adaptable example cybersecurity solutions demonstrating how to apply standards and best practices using commercially available technology.

LEARN MORE

Visit https://www.nccoe.nist.gov
nccoe@nist.gov
301-975-0200

NIST SPECIAL PUBLICATION 1800-19B

Trusted Cloud

Security Practice Guide for VMware Hybrid Cloud Infrastructure as a Service (IaaS) Environments

Volume B:
Approach, Architecture, and Security Characteristics

Michael Bartock, Murugiah Souppaya, and Karen Scarfone, NIST

Daniel Carroll and Robert Masten, Dell/EMC

Gina Scinta and Paul Massis, Gemalto

Hemma Prafullchandra and Jason Malnar, HyTrust

Harmeet Singh, IBM

Raghuram Yeluri, Intel

Tim Shea and Michael Dalton, RSA

Anthony Dukes, Carlos Phoenix, and Brenda Swarts, VMware

November 2018

PRELIMINARY DRAFT

This publication is available free of charge from:
https://www.nccoe.nist.gov/projects/building-blocks/trusted-cloud

DISCLAIMER

Certain commercial entities, equipment, products, or materials may be identified in this document in order to describe an experimental procedure or concept adequately. Such identification is not intended to imply recommendation or endorsement by NIST or NCCoE, nor is it intended to imply that the entities, equipment, products, or materials are necessarily the best available for the purpose.

National Institute of Standards and Technology Special Publication 1800-19B, Natl. Inst. Stand. Technol. Spec. Publ. 1800-19B, 53 pages, (November 2018), CODEN: NSPUE2

FEEDBACK

You can improve this document by contributing feedback.

Comments on this publication may be submitted to: trusted-cloud-nccoe@nist.gov.

Public comment period: November 20, 2018 through January 11, 2019

All comments are subject to release under the Freedom of Information Act (FOIA).

National Cybersecurity Center of Excellence
National Institute of Standards and Technology
100 Bureau Drive
Mailstop 2002
Gaithersburg, MD 20899
Email: nccoe@nist.gov

NATIONAL CYBERSECURITY CENTER OF EXCELLENCE

The National Cybersecurity Center of Excellence (NCCoE), a part of the National Institute of Standards and Technology (NIST), is a collaborative hub where industry organizations, government agencies, and academic institutions work together to address businesses' most pressing cybersecurity issues. This public-private partnership enables the creation of practical cybersecurity solutions for specific industries, as well as for broad, cross-sector technology challenges. Through consortia under Cooperative Research and Development Agreements (CRADAs), including technology partners—from Fortune 50 market leaders to smaller companies specializing in IT security—the NCCoE applies standards and best practices to develop modular, easily adaptable example cybersecurity solutions using commercially available technology. The NCCoE documents these example solutions in the NIST Special Publication 1800 series, which maps capabilities to the NIST Cybersecurity Framework and details the steps needed for another entity to recreate the example solution. The NCCoE was established in 2012 by NIST in partnership with the State of Maryland and Montgomery County, Md.

To learn more about the NCCoE, visit https://www.nccoe.nist.gov/. To learn more about NIST, visit https://www.nist.gov.

NIST CYBERSECURITY PRACTICE GUIDES

NIST Cybersecurity Practice Guides (Special Publication Series 1800) target specific cybersecurity challenges in the public and private sectors. They are practical, user-friendly guides that facilitate the adoption of standards-based approaches to cybersecurity. They show members of the information security community how to implement example solutions that help them align more easily with relevant standards and best practices, and provide users with the materials lists, configuration files, and other information they need to implement a similar approach.

The documents in this series describe example implementations of cybersecurity practices that businesses and other organizations may voluntarily adopt. These documents do not describe regulations or mandatory practices, nor do they carry statutory authority.

ABSTRACT

A *cloud workload* is an abstraction of the actual instance of a functional application that is virtualized or containerized to include compute, storage, and network resources. Organizations need to be able to monitor, track, apply, and enforce their security and privacy policies on their cloud workloads, based on business requirements, in a consistent, repeatable, and automated way. The goal of this project is to develop a trusted cloud solution that will demonstrate how trusted compute pools leveraging hardware roots of trust can provide the necessary security capabilities. These capabilities not only provide assurance that cloud workloads are running on trusted hardware and in a trusted geolocation or logical boundary, but also improve the protections for the data in the workloads and in the data flows between workloads. The example solution leverages modern commercial off-the-shelf technology and cloud services to address a particular use case scenario: lifting and shifting a typical multi-tier application between an organization-controlled private cloud and a hybrid/public cloud over the internet.

KEYWORDS

cloud technology; compliance; cybersecurity; privacy; trusted compute pools

DRAFT

ACKNOWLEDGMENTS

The Technology Partners/Collaborators who participated in this build submitted their capabilities in response to a notice in the Federal Register. Respondents with relevant capabilities or product components were invited to sign a Cooperative Research and Development Agreement (CRADA) with NIST, allowing them to participate in a consortium to build this example solution. We worked with:

Technology Partner/Collaborator	Build Involvement
Dell EMC	Server, storage, and networking hardware
Gemalto	Hardware security module (HSM) for storing keys
HyTrust	Asset tagging and policy enforcement, workload and storage encryption, and data scanning
IBM	Public cloud environment with IBM provisioned servers
Intel	Intel processors in the Dell EMC servers
RSA	Multifactor authentication, network traffic monitoring, and dashboard and reporting
VMware	Compute, storage, and network virtualization capabilities

Contents

46 ## List of Figures

64 List of Tables

1   Summary

Building on previous work documented in National Institute of Standards and Technology Interagency Report (NISTIR) 7904, *Trusted Geolocation in the Cloud: Proof of Concept Implementation* [1], the goal of the project is to expand upon the security capabilities provided by trusted compute pools in a hybrid cloud model, including the following capabilities:

- single pane of glass for the management and monitoring of cloud workloads, including software configurations and vulnerabilities

- data protection and encryption key management enforcement focused on trust-based and geolocation-based/resource pools, and secure migration of cloud workloads

- key management and keystore controlled by the organization, not the cloud service provider

- persistent data flow segmentation before and after the trust-based and geolocation-based/resource pools secure migration

- industry sector and/or organizational business compliance enforcement for regulated workloads between the on-premises private and hybrid/public clouds

These additional capabilities will not only provide assurance that cloud workloads are running on trusted hardware and in a trusted geolocation or logical boundary, but also will improve the protections for the data in the workloads and in the data flows between workloads.

1.1   Challenge

Cloud services can provide organizations, including federal agencies, with the opportunity to increase the flexibility, availability, resiliency, and scalability of cloud services, which the organizations can, in turn, use to increase security, privacy, efficiency, responsiveness, innovation, and competitiveness. However, many organizations, especially those in regulated sectors like finance and healthcare, face additional security and privacy challenges when adopting cloud services.

Cloud platform hardware and software are evolving to take advantage of the latest hardware and software features, and there are hundreds or thousands of virtualized or containerized workloads that are spun up, scaled out, moved around, and shut down at any instant, based on business requirements. In such environments, organizations want to be able to monitor, track, apply, and enforce policies on the workloads, based on business requirements, in a consistent, repeatable, and automated way. In other words, organizations want to maintain consistent security protections and to have visibility and control for their workloads across on-premises private clouds and third-party hybrid/public clouds in order to meet their security and compliance requirements.

This is further complicated by organizations' need to comply with security and privacy laws applicable to the information that they collect, transmit, or hold, which may change depending on whose information it is (e.g., Europeans citizens under the General Data Protection Regulation), what kind of information it

103   is (e.g., health information compared to financial information), and in what state or country the
104   information is located. Additionally, an organization must be able to meets its own policies by
105   implementing appropriate controls dictated by its risk-based decisions about the necessary security and
106   privacy of its information.

107   Because laws in one location may conflict with an organization's policies or mandates (e.g., laws,
108   regulations), an organization may decide that it needs to restrict the type of cloud servers it uses, based
109   on the state or country. Thus, the core impediments to broader adoption of cloud technologies are the
110   abilities of an organization to protect its information and virtual assets in the cloud, and to have
111   sufficient visibility into that information so that it can conduct oversight and ensure that it and its cloud
112   provider are complying with applicable laws and business practices.

113   In addition, there are technical challenges and architectural decisions that have to be made when
114   connecting two disparate clouds. An important consideration revolves around the type of wide area
115   network connecting the on-premises private cloud and the hybrid/public cloud, because it may impact
116   the latency of the workloads and the security posture of the management plane across the two
117   infrastructures.

1.2 Solution
118

119   The project involves collaborating with industry partners to design, engineer, and build solutions
120   leveraging commercial off-the-shelf technology and cloud services to deliver a trusted cloud
121   implementation. This implementation will allow organizations in regulated industries to leverage the
122   flexibility, availability, resiliency, and scalability of cloud services while complying with applicable
123   requirements, such as the Federal Information Security Modernization Act (FISMA), the Payment Card
124   Industry Data Security Standard (PCI DSS), and the Health Insurance Portability and Accountability Act
125   (HIPAA), as well as industry-neutral voluntary frameworks like the National Institute of Standards and
126   Technology (NIST) Cybersecurity Framework. The technology stack will include modern hardware and
127   software that can be leveraged to support the described use cases and to ease the adoption of cloud
128   technology.

129   The example implementation is for a hybrid cloud use case, enabling an organization to lift and shift a
130   typical multi-tier application between a private cloud stack located in the National Cybersecurity Center
131   of Excellence (NCCoE) data center and the IBM public cloud over the public internet.

1.3 Benefits

- Organizations will be able to maintain consistent security and privacy protections for information across cloud platforms; dictate how different information is protected, such as having stronger protection for more-sensitive information; and retain visibility into how their information is protected, to ensure consistent compliance with legal and business requirements.

- Technical staff will learn how to utilize commercial off-the-shelf technology and cloud services, to achieve trusted cloud implementations that protect cloud workloads and that support compliance initiatives.

- Senior management and information security officers will be motivated to use trusted cloud technologies.

2 How to Use This Guide

This is a preliminary draft of Volume B of a NIST Cybersecurity Practice Guide currently under development. This draft is not yet complete because the build of the trusted cloud example implementation at the NCCoE is ongoing. This draft is provided to reviewers who would like to follow the ongoing work and stay informed on the progress of the project. **Organizations should not attempt to implement this preliminary draft.**

When completed, this NIST Cybersecurity Practice Guide will demonstrate a standards-based reference design and provide users with the information they need to replicate the trusted compute pools in a hybrid cloud model that provide expanded security capabilities. This reference design will be modular and can be deployed in whole or in part.

This guide will contain three volumes:

- NIST Special Publication (SP) 1800-19A: *Executive Summary*

- NIST SP 1800-19B: *Approach, Architecture, and Security Characteristics* – what we built and why **(you are here)**

- NIST SP 1800-19C: *How-To Guides* – instructions for building the example solution

Depending on your role in your organization, you might use this guide in different ways:

Business decision makers, including chief security and technology officers, will be interested in the *Executive Summary, NIST SP 1800-19A*, which describes the following topics:

- challenges enterprises face in protecting cloud workloads in hybrid cloud models

- example solution built at the NCCoE

- benefits of adopting the example solution

163 **Technology or security program managers** who are concerned with how to identify, understand, assess,
164 and mitigate risk will be interested in this part of the guide, *NIST SP 1800-19B,* which describes what we
165 did and why. The following sections will be of particular interest:

166   ▪   Section 3.4.3, Risk, provides a description of the risk analysis we performed

167   ▪   Appendix A, Mappings, maps the security characteristics of this example solution to
168   cybersecurity standards and best practices

169 You might share the *Executive Summary, NIST SP 1800-19A,* with your leadership team members to help
170 them understand the importance of adopting standards-based trusted compute pools in a hybrid cloud
171 model that provide expanded security capabilities.

172 **Information Technology (IT) professionals** who want to implement an approach like this will find the
173 whole practice guide useful. You will be able to use the How-To portion of the guide, *NIST SP 1800-19C,*
174 to replicate all or parts of the build being created in our lab. The How-To portion of the guide will
175 provide specific product installation, configuration, and integration instructions for implementing the
176 example solution. We will not recreate the product manufacturers' documentation, which is generally
177 widely available. Rather, we will show how we incorporated the products together in our environment
178 to create an example solution.

179 This guide will assume that IT professionals have experience implementing security products within the
180 enterprise. While we are using a suite of commercial products to address this challenge, this guide does
181 not endorse these particular products. Your organization can adopt this solution or one that adheres to
182 these guidelines in whole, or you can use this guide as a starting point for tailoring and implementing
183 parts of a trusted cloud implementation leveraging commercial off-the-shelf technology. Your
184 organization's security experts should identify the products that will best integrate with your existing
185 tools and IT system infrastructure. We hope that you will seek products that are congruent with
186 applicable standards and best practices. Section 4.2, Technologies, lists the products we are using and
187 maps them to the cybersecurity controls provided by this reference solution.

188 A NIST Cybersecurity Practice Guide does not describe "the" solution, but a possible solution. This is a
189 draft guide. We seek feedback on its contents and welcome your input. Comments, suggestions, and
190 success stories will improve subsequent versions of this guide. Please contribute your thoughts to
191 trusted-cloud-nccoe@nist.gov.

192 2.1 Typographical Conventions

193 The following table presents typographic conventions used in this volume.

Typeface/Symbol	Meaning	Example
Italics	file names and path names; references to documents that are not hyperlinks; new terms; and placeholders	For detailed definitions of terms, see the *NCCoE Glossary*.
Bold	names of menus, options, command buttons, and fields	Choose **File > Edit**.
`Monospace`	command-line input, on-screen computer output, sample code examples, and status codes	`mkdir`
`Monospace Bold`	command-line user input contrasted with computer output	`service sshd start`
blue text	link to other parts of the document, a web URL, or an email address	All publications from NIST's NCCoE are available at https://www.nccoe.nist.gov.

194 3 Approach

195 The NCCoE invited technology providers to participate in demonstrating a proposed approach for
196 implementing trusted resource pools leveraging commercial off-the-shelf technology and cloud services
197 to aggregate trusted systems and segregate them from untrusted resources. This would result in the
198 separation of higher-value, more-sensitive workloads from commodity application and data workloads
199 in an infrastructure as a service (IaaS) deployment model. In this project, the example implementation
200 involves securely migrating—"lifting and shifting"—a multi-tier application from an organization-
201 controlled private cloud to a hybrid/public cloud over the internet. The implementation automatically,
202 and with assurance, restricts cloud workloads to servers meeting selected characteristics. It also
203 provides the ability to determine the security posture of a cloud workload at any time through
204 continuous monitoring, no matter the cloud or the cloud server.

205 The NCCoE prepared a Federal Register notice [2] seeking technology providers to provide products
206 and/or expertise to compose prototypes that include commodity servers with hardware cryptographic
207 modules; commodity network switches; hypervisors; operating systems (OSs); application containers;
208 attestation servers; orchestration and management servers; database servers; directory servers;
209 software-defined networks; data encryption and key management servers; and cloud services.

210 Cooperative Research and Development Agreements (CRADAs) were established with qualified
211 respondents, and "build teams" were assembled.

212 The following actions have been, or will be, performed by the build teams:

213 ▪ fleshing out the initial architecture and composing the collaborators' components into
214 demonstration prototypes

215 ▪ documenting the architecture and design implementation, including the steps taken to install
216 and configure each component of the demonstration environment

217 ▪ conducting security and functional testing of the demonstration environment, and then
218 conducting and documenting the results of a risk assessment and a security characteristics
219 analysis

220 ▪ working with industry collaborators to suggest future considerations

221 3.1 Audience

222 This guide is intended for cloud computing practitioners, system integrators, IT managers, security
223 managers, IT architects, and others interested in practical, effective implementations of trusted cloud
224 technologies that can reduce risk and satisfy existing system security requirements.

225 3.2 Scope

226 The scope of this project is the usage of hybrid/public clouds and on-premises private clouds to securely
227 host an organization's own workloads in an IaaS deployment model. The project is intended to be
228 particularly useful to organizations in regulated industries, but it should be of use to organizations in any
229 industry and sector.

230 3.3 Assumptions

231 This project is guided by the following assumptions:

232 ▪ Organizations implementing this solution are responsible for providing core infrastructure
233 services, including Microsoft Active Directory, certificate services, Domain Name System (DNS),
234 Dynamic Host Configuration Protocol (DHCP), Network Time Protocol (NTP), Simple Mail
235 Transfer Protocol (SMTP), Simple Network Management Protocol (SNMP), and logging services.

236 ▪ Organizations should already have their physical infrastructure configured to be fault tolerant.

237 ▪ Organizations should work with their cloud service provider, legal team, and others as needed to
238 have the necessary agreements in place about responsibilities.

239 ▪ Federal agencies will need to choose hybrid/public clouds that are Federal Risk and
240 Authorization Management Program (FedRAMP) certified. Other industry sectors should follow
241 their sector-specific cloud service certification program.

242 ▪ Organizations will need to implement and manage all security controls that their cloud service
243   provider is not formally responsible for implementing and maintaining on their behalf.

244 ▪ Organizations will need to ensure that the VMware Validated Design meets their requirements
245   for availability, manageability, performance, recoverability, and security.

246 ▪ Organizations will need to ensure that they have identified all applicable compliance
247   requirements.

248 ▪ Organizations should have trained and qualified staff to architect, secure, and operate the
249   solution stack.

3.4 Risk Assessment

251 NIST SP 800-30, *Guide for Conducting Risk Assessments* states that a risk is "a measure of the extent to
252 which an entity is threatened by a potential circumstance or event, and typically a function of (i) the
253 adverse impacts that would arise if the circumstance or event occurs and (ii) the likelihood of
254 occurrence." The guide further defines risk assessment as "the process of identifying, estimating, and
255 prioritizing risks to organizational operations (including mission, functions, image, reputation),
256 organizational assets, individuals, other organizations, and the Nation, resulting from the operation of
257 an information system. Part of risk management incorporates threat and vulnerability analyses, and
258 considers mitigations provided by security controls planned or in place."[3]

259 The NCCoE recommends that any discussion of risk management, particularly at the enterprise level,
260 begin with a comprehensive review of NIST SP 800-37, *Guide for Applying the Risk Management
261 Framework to Federal Information Systems* [4] for the United States (U.S.) government public sector;
262 private-sector risk management frameworks (RMFs), such as International Organization for
263 Standardization (ISO) 31000 [5], Committee of Sponsoring Organizations of the Treadway Commission
264 (COSO) Enterprise Risk Management – Integrating with Strategy and Performance (2017) [6], and Factor
265 Analysis of Information Risk (FAIR) [7]; or sector-agnostic frameworks, such as the NIST Cybersecurity
266 Framework [8]—material that is available to the public. The RMF guidance, as a whole, proved to be
267 invaluable in giving us a baseline to assess risks, from which we developed the project, the security
268 characteristics of the build, and this guide.

3.4.1 Threats

270 Table 3-1 lists examples of common threats associated with the hybrid cloud usage scenario of this
271 project, where two clouds under the control of different providers are linked together so that workloads
272 can be moved between them. This list of threats is not meant to be comprehensive.

273   **Table 3-1 Common Threats Associated with Hybrid Cloud Usage**

Threat/Attack Type	Example	Addressed by Solution
Threats Against Cloud Infrastructure		
Physical threat against data center (e.g., natural disaster, cooling system failure)	A regional power outage necessitates shutting down servers at one data center location.	Have adequate environmental controls in place for the data center, such as backup power, heating and cooling mechanisms, and fire detection and suppression systems. Be prepared to automatically shift workloads to another suitable location at any time. The enterprise data center infrastructure team or cloud service operators are responsible for providing these mechanisms.
Tampering with server firmware (e.g., Basic Input/ Output System [BIOS])	An unapproved change management control or a malicious insider gains physical access to a server in the data center and alters its BIOS configuration to disable its security protections.	Use physical security controls to restrict data center access to authorized personnel only. Monitor data center access at all times. Detect changes by taking an integrity measurement of the BIOS at boot and comparing it with a previous measurement taken in a "clean room" environment and configured as a good known BIOS.
Threats Against Cloud Management		
Tampering with a virtual machine manager (VMM)	An unapproved change management control, a malicious insider, or an external attacker with stolen administrator credentials reuses them to gain access to the VMM and install malicious code.	Detect changes to the VMM by taking an integrity measurement of the kernel and specific vSphere Installation Bundles (VIBs) at boot and comparing it with previous measurements taken in a "clean room" environment and configured as a good known host (GKH).

Threat/Attack Type	Example	Addressed by Solution
Unauthorized administrator-level or service-level access	An external attacker steals an administrator account password and reuses it to gain access to a file.	Enforce strong authentication, including two-factor authentication with a cryptographic token, for all administrative and service access to cloud workloads, VMMs, and other management systems. Allow only administrators to manage the systems they have a need to administer, by enforcing least privilege and separation of duties. Monitor the use of administrator and service credentials at all times, log all access attempts, and alert when suspicious activity is observed.
Administrative changes (accidental or malicious) that are destructive	An administrator accidentally deletes a virtualized domain controller.	Enforce secondary approval workflow for specific assets and/or administrative operations, to implement the "four-eyes" principle for highly sensitive systems and/or operations.
Intentional or accidental configuration changes that violate hardening best practices	Upgrading an authorized application inadvertently wipes out existing application configuration settings.	Continuously monitor all configuration changes on all components. Run regularly scheduled assessments and remediations with customized hardening templates to remain in compliance with configuration hardening best practices.
Unauthorized access to secret cryptographic keys	An attacker takes advantage of a weak key management protocol implementation to intercept unprotected keys being distributed to virtual machines (VMs).	Provide Federal Information Processing Standard (FIPS) 140-2-validated, Key Management Interoperability Protocol (KMIP)-compliant key management services for cryptographic functions that operate in a hardware security module (HSM) to safeguard sensitive key materials.
Threats Against Cloud Workload Storage, Execution, and Use		
Running a cloud workload within an untrusted environment or location	A cloud administrator may respond to an impending maintenance disruption by moving cloud workloads to cloud servers in other locations.	Allow cloud workloads to execute only on a physical server that is known to be good (i.e., not tampered with) and is within an authorized geolocation.

Threat/Attack Type	Example	Addressed by Solution
Unauthorized access from one cloud workload to another within a cloud	A user of one cloud workload connects to another organization's cloud workload and exploits vulnerabilities in it to gain unauthorized access.	Establish network boundaries through dedicated virtual local area networks (VLANs) leveraging automated access control lists (ACLs). Use Institute of Electrical and Electronics Engineers (IEEE) 802.1Q VLAN tagging for network traffic within the cloud data center, so that only traffic tagged with a server's unique VLAN identifier is routed to or from that server.
Unauthorized movement within the cloud environment from a compromised cloud workload (e.g., lateral movement)	A cloud workload is compromised, and the attacker has full privileged access to the system. The attacker tries to move laterally to discover sensitive resources and escalate privileges to gain greater access to the environment.	Use software-defined technology and user privilege segmentation to whitelist the network communications and access rights.
Intentional or accidental exposure of sensitive data	An administrator copies a cloud workload file to an unauthorized location.	Encrypt cloud workloads at rest. Use end-to-end encryption with mutual authentication when moving a workload from one location to another.
Unauthorized access to files containing sensitive data	A malicious insider misuses OS access to copy a file.	Scan filesystems for sensitive data, categorize the discovered files, monitor all access to those files, and report on that access. Enforce access controls that prevent different cloud provider administrators of cloud workloads from accessing sensitive applications and data drives.

274 3.4.2 Vulnerabilities

275 The primary areas of concern are software flaws and misconfigurations at all levels of the architecture:
276 low-level services (compute, storage, network), VMMs, OSs, and applications, including cloud workload
277 management, VMM management, and other management tools. Related to these concerns is the need
278 to ensure that the same security policies are being enforced within both clouds for the cloud workloads
279 to eliminate some vulnerabilities and mitigate others.

280 Some examples of vulnerabilities that might be particularly impactful if exploited are listed below:

- 281 cryptographic keys being stored or transmitted without being strongly encrypted

- 282 cloud workloads being migrated without performing mutual authentication of the clouds or
- 283 verifying the integrity of the migrated workload

- 284 weak administrator or service account credentials that are highly susceptible to theft and
- 285 unauthorized reuse

- 286 access controls that do not enforce the principles of least privilege and separation of duties

287 3.4.3 Risk

288 The proposed solution implements several layers of controls to protect cloud workloads while they
289 reside within clouds and while they are migrated from one cloud to another. The cloud workloads are
290 still vulnerable. For example, an unknown software flaw in a cloud workload's software, or in the VMM
291 underlying that workload, could be exploited, potentially compromising the workload itself. There are
292 always residual risks for cloud workloads. The proposed solution includes only technical controls;
293 therefore, risk involving the solution's physical environment, people (e.g., users, administrators),
294 processes, and other non-technical items will also need to be addressed.

295 4 Architecture

296 At a high level, the trusted cloud architecture has three main pieces: a private cloud hosted at the
297 NCCoE, an instance of the public IBM Cloud Secure Virtualization (ICSV), and an Internet Protocol
298 Security (IPsec) virtual private network (VPN) that connects the two clouds to form a hybrid cloud.
299 Figure 4-1 provides a simplified diagram of the architecture.

300 The private on-premises cloud at the NCCoE consists of the following components:

- 301 HSM for storing keys by Gemalto

- 302 server, storage, and networking hardware by Dell EMC

- 303 Intel processors in the Dell EMC servers

- 304 compute, storage, and network virtualization capabilities by VMware

- 305 asset tagging and policy enforcement, workload and storage encryption, and data scanning by
- 306 HyTrust

- 307 multifactor authentication, network traffic monitoring, and dashboard and reporting by RSA

308 The ICSV instance consists of the following components:

- 309 IBM-provisioned servers with Intel processors

- 310 compute, storage, network virtualization with VMware components

311   ▪   asset tagging and policy enforcement, and workload and storage encryption with HyTrust
312   components

313 The IPSec VPN established between the two clouds allows them to be part of the same management
314 domain, so that each component can be managed and utilized in the same fashion, which creates one
315 hybrid cloud. The workloads can be shifted or live-migrated between the two sites.

316 **Figure 4-1 High-Level Solution Architecture**

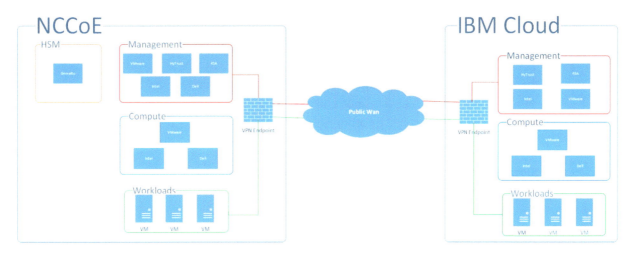

317

4.1   Architecture Components

319 Within the high-level architecture, there are four main components that comprise the trusted cloud
320 build:

321   ▪   **HSM component:** This build utilizes HSMs to store sensitive keys within the environment. One
322   set of HSMs is used for the domain's root and issuing transport layer security (TLS) certificate
323   authorities (CAs), while another HSM is used to protect keys that are used to encrypt workloads.
324   The HSM component is deployed in the private cloud at the NCCoE, and network access is
325   strictly limited to only the machines that need to communicate with it.

326   ▪   **Management component:** The identical functional management components are instantiated
327   across the NCCoE private cloud and the ICSV public cloud instance. The single management
328   console is used to operate the virtual infrastructure hosting the tenant workloads. At a
329   minimum, each management component consists of hardware utilizing Intel processors,
330   VMware running the virtualization stack, HyTrust providing the asset tagging policy enforcement
331   aspect, and RSA providing network-visibility, dashboard, and reporting capabilities. The
332   management components on each site are connected through the IPsec VPN to represent one
333   logical management element.

334   ▪   **Compute component:** Both sites of the hybrid cloud include similar compute components. The
335   compute components host the tenant workload VMs. Asset tagging is provisioned on the

336   compute servers so that policy can be assigned and enforced to ensure that tenant workloads
337   reside on servers that meet specific regulatory compliance requirements. At a minimum, each
338   compute component consists of hardware utilizing Intel processors, and VMware running the
339   virtualization stack. The compute components on each site are connected through the IPsec VPN
340   so that workloads can be migrated between the two sites.

341   ▪ **Workload component:** Both sites of the hybrid cloud have similar workload components. The
342   workload components include VMs, data storage, and networks owned and operated by the
343   tenant and data owner. Policies are applied to the workloads to ensure that they can run only
344   on servers that meet specific requirements, such as asset tag policies.

4.2 Technologies

346   We built the proposed solution by using products from vendors who have established CRADAs with the
347   NCCoE for this project. The NCCoE does not endorse or recommend these products. Each organization
348   should determine if these products, or other products on the market with similar capabilities, best meet
349   your own requirements and integrate well with your existing IT system infrastructure.

350   The following subsections describe the vendors and products that we used for our example solution.

4.2.1 Dell EMC

352   Dell EMC has developed a keen focus on building security into the product design versus bolting on
353   security after release. For this solution, Dell EMC provided enterprise and in-rack networking solutions,
354   Dell PowerEdge Servers to provide compute capabilities, and Dell EMC Unity unified storage for the
355   primary storage solutions.

356   Dell Networking solutions utilizing the OS9 OS and the Dell PowerEdge servers have gone through
357   rigorous testing and approval processes to be published on the Defense Information Systems Agency
358   (DISA) Approved Products List. This includes the inclusion of the Integrated Dell Remote Access
359   Controller, Lifecycle Controller, and connectivity to the OpenManage solution. This capability allows for
360   enterprise standardization of platform and switch configurations to enable NIST SP 800-53 security
361   controls [9].

362   Dell EMC Unity provides a robust unified storage solution with built-in security configuration that allows
363   for a simple enablement of platform hardening to meet DISA Security Technical Implementation Guide
364   (STIG) standards. The Dell EMC Unity solution OS is based on a derivative of SUSE Linux 12. Dell EMC, in
365   collaboration with DISA, performed extensive testing and development to ensure that Dell EMC Unity
366   meets the high standards that DISA has established for its Approved Product Listing.

367   Dell EMC provided implementation and consulting services to ensure that these components of the
368   overall solution were implemented to meet the proof-of-concept guidelines for a highly secured
369   infrastructure.

4.2.2 Gemalto

Gemalto's Enterprise and Cybersecurity business unit focuses on providing solutions for the encryption of data at rest and data in motion, secure storage and management of encryption keys through the use of HSMs and centralized key management, and controlling access by using multifactor authentication and identity access management across cloud, virtual, and on-premises environments.

SafeNet Hardware Security Modules provide the highest level of security by always storing cryptographic keys in hardware. SafeNet HSMs provide a secure cryptographic foundation, as the keys never leave the intrusion-resistant, tamper-evident, FIPS-validated appliance. Because all cryptographic operations occur within the HSM, strong access controls prevent unauthorized users from accessing sensitive cryptographic material.

The SafeNet Luna Universal Serial Bus (USB) HSM is a small form-factor USB-attached HSM that is used as a root of trust for storing root cryptographic keys in an offline key storage device.

The SafeNet Luna Network HSM (Versions 6 and 7) is a network-attached HSM protecting encryption keys used by applications in on-premises, virtual, and cloud environments. The HSM has more than 400 integrations. For this project, SafeNet Luna Network HSM 7 is the root of trust for Microsoft Active Directory Certificate Services (ADCS) used to issue TLS certificates. SafeNet Luna Network HSM 6 is integrated as the root of trust for HyTrust KeyControl (HTKC) via the KMIP key management service.

The SafeNet Backup HSM ensures that sensitive cryptographic material remains strongly protected in hardware, even when not being used. You can back up and duplicate keys securely to the SafeNet Backup HSM for safekeeping in case of emergency, failure, or disaster.

4.2.3 HyTrust

HyTrust helps make cloud infrastructure more trustworthy for those organizations pursuing a multi-cloud approach, by delivering a critical set of capabilities required to proactively secure workloads wherever they reside. The HyTrust Cloud Security Policy Framework (CloudSPF) allows organizations to automate the creation, application, and enforcement of security and compliance policies for private, hybrid, and public cloud workloads, including three critical attributes of the workload—people, data, and infrastructure. HyTrust CloudSPF is supported by a portfolio of five solutions that deliver the functionality needed to enable policy-driven security and automated compliance of workloads in multi-cloud environments—including securing data and ensuring data privacy, preventing privileged admin misuse, automating compliance tasks, securing multi-tenant environments, and more. The five solutions are as follows:

- **HyTrust CloudControl (HTCC):** Workload Security Policy Enforcement and Compliance: Key capabilities help organizations protect their virtualized infrastructures with authentication, authorization, and auditing. Better visibility and control simplify compliance and accelerate further virtualization and data center transformation. CloudControl functionality includes two-

| 405 | factor authentication, secondary approval workflows, advanced role-based and object-based |
| 406 | access controls, audit-quality logging, and hypervisor hardening. |

407	▪ **HyTrust DataControl (HTDC):** Workload Encryption and Integrated Key Management: Provides
408	strong data-at-rest encryption for workloads in any cloud, along with easy-to-deploy key
409	management that organizations control—whether workloads are running in a private cloud
410	powered by vSphere or in a hybrid/public cloud like IBM Cloud, Microsoft Azure, or Amazon
411	Web Services (AWS)—throughout the entire workload life cycle. DataControl also supports the
412	highest levels of availability by offering the ability to rekey workloads without taking
413	applications offline.

414	▪ **HTKC:** Workload Encryption Key Management: Simplifies the process of key management for
415	workloads that do not require sophisticated policy-based key management, but that need to
416	scale to enterprise-level performance. Organizations retain full ownership of encryption keys
417	with policy-based controls to protect data and to meet compliance requirements. KeyControl
418	works with both DataControl and third-party encryption solutions, such as VMware vSphere VM
419	Encryption and vSAN.

420	▪ **HyTrust CloudAdvisor (HTCA):** Data Discovery and Classification Across Virtual Machines and
421	Backups: Provides complete visibility into data stored within each workload and associates this
422	information with whomever is interacting with it and when. CloudAdvisor defines policies to
423	automatically discover the data that is valuable; detect anomalous user access behaviors; and
424	defend an organization against careless exposure, data loss, malicious users, and regulatory
425	noncompliance.

426	▪ **HyTrust BoundaryControl (HTBC):** Workload Placement Policies, Data Geo-Fencing, and
427	Location-Aware Encryption: Enables administrators to set policies so that workloads can run
428	only on proven, trusted hosts that are physically located within the defined parameters.
429	BoundaryControl's foundation is rooted in Intel Trusted Execution Technology (Intel TXT), which
430	provides processor-level attestation of the hardware, BIOS, and hypervisor. Administrators can
431	also assign labels that bind workloads to run only in predefined locations. Also, encryption
432	policies can be applied to ensure that data is never decrypted outside the defined
433	parameters/boundary.

434 4.2.4 IBM

435	ICSV combines the power of IBM Cloud bare-metal servers, VMware virtualization and management
436	applications (IBM Cloud for VMware – vCenter Server [vCS]), HyTrust security virtual appliances
437	(HTCC/HTDC), Intel TXT, and Intel Trusted Platform Module (TPM). This service provides enhanced
438	security capabilities, utilizing automation from deployment to ongoing management.

439	ICSV allows clients to set, apply, and automate the enforcement of workload governance policies to
440	meet their security needs for critical workloads and to support regulatory or industry compliance
441	requirements through continuous monitoring and real-time reporting. ICSV gives clients visibility of
442	physical servers across any virtualized infrastructure, so that they can ensure that only authorized

443 servers in authorized locations handle sensitive workloads. In turn, clients can better enforce only
444 authorized administrator actions and can help make sure that all requested actions—whether approved
445 or denied—are logged for reporting and compliance. With this type of control and visibility, clients can
446 more effectively reduce risk and increase security, allowing them to address in-house security needs as
447 well as compliance requirements for mission-critical business operations. This means that they can now
448 take full advantage of the benefits of cloud computing while maintaining the strongest levels of data
449 protection, visibility, and auditing necessary to protect the business.

450 IBM Cloud bare-metal servers function as the hardware foundation of this solution. The IBM Cloud
451 service allows customers to provision bare-metal servers according to their needs. In contrast to
452 environments with typical cloud-based VMs, customers have control over these bare-metal servers.
453 Customers can specify the servers' OS, security configuration, and other configuration aspects, including
454 modifying server BIOS settings and deploying various hypervisors. The bare-metal servers are built with
455 Intel Xeon processors, which come equipped with Intel TXT and TPM technologies that enable trusted
456 compute pools (via HTCC) for workloads and data. The servers also take advantage of Intel technologies,
457 such as Intel Advanced Encryption Standard – New Instructions (Intel AES-NI), and other cryptographic
458 technologies to enhance and accelerate encryption (via HTDC).

459 The ICSV solution complements the IBM Cloud for VMware – vCS offering by providing security services.
460 ICSV takes advantage of the infrastructure automation jointly developed by IBM and VMware. This
461 advanced automation supports the deployment and integration of Intel and HyTrust technologies with
462 the vCS from VMware, so that IBM clients can continue to use familiar tools to manage their workloads
463 without having to retool or refactor applications. IBM Cloud for VMware – vCS provides the
464 virtualization of compute, storage, and networking, providing a software-defined data center.

4.2.5 Intel

466 The Intel Data Center Group (DCG) is at the heart of Intel's transformation from a personal computer
467 (PC) company to a company that runs the cloud and billions of smart, connected computing devices. The
468 data center is the underpinning for every data-driven service, from artificial intelligence to 5G to high-
469 performance computing, and DCG delivers the products and technologies—spanning software,
470 processors, storage, input/output (I/O), security and networking solutions—that fuel cloud,
471 communications, enterprise, and government data centers around the world.

472 Intel TXT provides hardware-based security technologies that address the increasing and evolving
473 security threats across physical and virtual infrastructures by complementing runtime protections, such
474 as anti-virus software. Intel TXT also can play a role in meeting government and industry regulations and
475 data protection standards by providing a hardware-based method of verification that is useful in
476 compliance efforts. Intel TXT is specifically designed to harden platforms from the emerging threats of
477 hypervisor attacks, BIOS, or other firmware attacks; malicious root kit installations; or other software-
478 based attacks. Intel TXT increases protection by allowing greater control of the launch stack through a

479   Measured Launch Environment (MLE) and enabling isolation in the boot process. More specifically, it
480   extends the Virtual Machine Extensions (VMX) environment of Intel Virtualization Technology (Intel VT),
481   permitting a verifiably secure installation, launch, and use of a hypervisor or OS.

482   Intel Cloud Integrity Technology (Intel CIT) extends a hardware-based root of trust up through the cloud
483   solution stack to ensure the privacy and integrity of cloud platforms and workloads. Intel CIT secures
484   cloud-based workloads through workload placement, encryption, and launch control bound to the
485   hardware-rooted chain of trust. By using Intel TXT to measure server firmware and software
486   components during system launch, server configurations can be verified against tampering. Extending
487   this chain of trust, additional software components, hypervisors, VMs and containers can be similarly
488   attested and verified. By encrypting workload images and tying the decryption key to server hardware
489   using a Trusted Platform Module, final control over where a VM may or may not launch is given to the
490   customer, preventing unauthorized access and enabling data sovereignty. Intel CIT is the foundational
491   technology leveraged by HyTrust to provide boundary and data-control capabilities.

492   ## 4.2.6 RSA

493   RSA, a Dell Technologies business, offers business-driven security solutions that uniquely link business
494   context with security incidents, to help organizations manage digital risk and protect what matters most.
495   RSA's award-winning cybersecurity solutions are designed to effectively detect and respond to advanced
496   attacks; manage user identities and access; and reduce business risk, fraud, and cybercrime. RSA
497   protects millions of users around the world and helps more than 90 percent of the Fortune 500
498   companies to thrive in an uncertain, high-risk world.

499   The RSA NetWitness Platform is an evolved Security Information and Event Management (SIEM) and
500   threat-defense solution engineered to immediately identify high-risk threats on devices, in the cloud,
501   and across your virtual enterprise. It automates security processes to reduce attacker dwell time and
502   make analysts more efficient and effective.

503   The RSA SecurID Suite is an advanced multifactor authentication and identity governance solution. It
504   applies risk analytics and business context to provide users with convenient, secure access to any
505   application from any device, and to simplify day-to-day identity governance for administrators.

506   The RSA Archer Suite is a comprehensive integrated risk-management solution designed to empower
507   organizations of all sizes to manage multiple dimensions of risk on a single, configurable, and integrated
508   platform. It features a wide variety of use cases for IT risk management, operational risk management,
509   and much more.

DRAFT

4.2.7 VMware

VMware, Inc., a subsidiary of Dell Technologies, provides virtualization and cloud-infrastructure solutions enabling businesses to transform the way they build, deliver, and consume IT resources. VMware is an industry-leading virtualization software company empowering organizations to innovate by streamlining IT operations and modernizing the data center into an on-demand service by pooling IT assets and automating services. VMware products allow customers to manage IT resources across private, hybrid, and public clouds. VMware offers services to its customers, including modernizing data centers, integrating public clouds, empowering digital workspaces, and transforming security.

VMware Validated Design (VVD) 4.2 is a family of solutions for data center designs that span compute, storage, networking, and management, serving as a blueprint for your software-defined data center (SDDC) implementations. VVDs are designed by experts and are continuously improved based on feedback from real deployments. The design is continuously validated for scale and interoperability, ensuring that it remains valid. The VVD is a comprehensive design that includes a fully functional SDDC while remaining hardware agnostic. Each VVD comes with its own reference design, deployment, operations, and upgrade guides: *Architecture and Design: VMware Validated Design for Management and Workload Consolidation 4.2* [10], *Deployment for Region A: VMware Validated Design for Software-Defined Data Center 4.2* [11], *Operational Verification: VMware Validated Design for Software-Defined Data Center 4.2* [12], and *Planning and Preparation: VMware Validated Design for Software-Defined Data Center 4.2* [13].

The standard VVD for an SDDC is a design for a production-ready SDDC that can be single-region or dual-region. Each region is deployed on two workload domains, management and shared edge and compute. VMs are separated into a minimum of two vSphere clusters, one for management VMs and one for customer VMs. Each of these clusters has a minimum of four ESXi hosts and is managed by a dedicated vCS. Additional compute hosts or clusters can be added to scale the solution as needed.

The standard VVD for an SDDC consists of the following VMware products:

- VMware vSphere virtualizes and aggregates the underlying physical hardware resources across multiple systems and provides pools of virtual resources to the data center. VMware vSphere includes the following components:

  - VMware ESXi is a type-1 hypervisor that enables a virtualization layer run on physical servers that abstracts processor, memory, storage, and resources into multiple VMs.

  - The Platform Services Controller (PSC) Appliance provides common infrastructure services to the vSphere environment. Services include licensing, certificate management, and authentication with vCenter Single Sign-On.

  - VMware vCS Appliance is a management application that allows for the management of VMs and ESXi hosts centrally. The vSphere Web Client is used to access the vCS.

545   • vSAN is fully integrated hypervisor-converged storage software. vSAN creates a cluster of
546   server hard-disk drives and solid-state drives, and presents a flash-optimized, highly-
547   resilient, shared storage data store to ESXi hosts and VMs. vSAN allows you to control the
548   capacity, performance, and availability, on a per-VM basis, through the use of storage
549   policies.

550   ▪ NSX for vSphere (NSX-V) creates a network virtualization layer. All virtual networks are created
551   on top of this layer, which is an abstraction between the physical and virtual networks. Network
552   virtualization services include logical switches, logical routers, logical firewalls, and other
553   components. This design includes the following components:

554   • NSX Manager provides the centralized management plane for NSX-V and has a one-to-one
555   mapping to vCS workloads.

556   • The NSX Virtual Switch is based on the vSphere Distributed Switch (VDS), with additional
557   components to enable rich services. The add-on NSX components include kernel modules
558   (VIBs) that run within the hypervisor kernel and that provide services, such as distributed
559   logical routers (DLRs), distributed firewalls (DFWs), and Virtual Extensible Local Area
560   Network (VXLAN) capabilities.

561   • NSX logical switches create logically abstracted segments to which tenant VMs can be
562   connected. NSX logical switches provide the ability to spin up isolated logical networks with
563   the same flexibility and agility that exist with VMs. Endpoints, both virtual and physical, can
564   connect to logical segments and establish connectivity independently from their physical
565   location in the data center network.

566   • The universal distributed logical router (UDLR) in NSX-V is optimized for forwarding in the
567   virtualized space (between VMs, on VXLAN-backed or VLAN-backed port groups).

568   • VXLAN Tunnel Endpoints (VTEPs) are instantiated within the VDS to which the ESXi hosts
569   that are prepared for NSX-V are connected. VTEPs are responsible for encapsulating VXLAN
570   traffic as frames in User Datagram Protocol (UDP) packets and for the corresponding
571   decapsulation. VTEPs exchange packets with other VTEPs.

572   • The primary function of the NSX Edge Services Gateway (ESG) is north-south
573   communication, but it also offers support for Layer 2; Layer 3; perimeter firewall; load
574   balancing; and other services, such as Secure Sockets Layer (SSL) VPN and DHCP relay.

575   ▪ vRealize Operations Manager (vROPS) tracks and analyzes the operation of multiple data
576   sources in the SDDC by using specialized analytic algorithms. These algorithms help vROPS learn
577   and predict the behavior of every object that it monitors. Users access this information by using
578   views, reports, and dashboards.

579   ▪ vRealize Log Insight (vRLI) provides real-time log management and log analysis with machine-
580   learning-based intelligent grouping, high-performance searching, and troubleshooting across
581   physical, virtual, and cloud environments.

582 ▪ vRealize Automation (vRA) provides the self-service provisioning, IT services delivery, and life-
583 cycle management of cloud services across a wide range of multivendor, virtual, physical, and
584 cloud platforms, through a flexible and robust distributed architecture.

585 ▪ vRealize Orchestrator (vRO) provides the automation of complex tasks by allowing for a quick
586 and easy design and deployment of scalable workflows. It automates management and
587 operational tasks across both VMware and third-party applications, such as service desks,
588 change management, and IT asset management systems.

589 ▪ vRealize Business for Cloud (vRB) automates cloud costing, consumption analysis, and
590 comparison, delivering the insight that you need for efficiently deploying and managing cloud
591 environments. vRB tracks and manages the costs of private and public cloud resources from a
592 single dashboard.

593 ▪ VMware Site Recovery Manager (optional, depends on failover site) is disaster-recovery
594 software that enables application availability and mobility across sites with policy-based
595 management, non-disruptive testing, and automated orchestration. Site Recovery Manager
596 administrators perform frequent non-disruptive testing to ensure IT disaster-recovery
597 predictability and compliance. Site Recovery Manager enables fast and reliable recovery by
598 using fully automated workflows.

599 ▪ vSphere Replication (vR) (optional, depends on failover site) is a hypervisor-based, asynchronous
600 replication solution for vSphere VMs. It is fully integrated with the VMware vCS and the vSphere
601 Web Client. vR delivers flexible, reliable, and cost-efficient replication to enable data protection
602 and disaster recovery for VMs.

4.2.8 Products and Technologies Summary

604 Table 4-1 lists all of the products and technologies that we incorporated in the proposed solution, and
605 maps each of them to the Cybersecurity Framework subcategories and the NIST SP 800-53 Revision 4
606 controls that the proposed solution helps address. Note that this is **not** a listing of every subcategory or
607 control that each product supports, uses for its own internal purposes, etc., but is a listing of those that
608 are being offered by the solution. For example, a component might be designed based on the principle
609 of least privilege for its internal functioning, but this component is not used to enforce the principle of
610 least privilege on access to cloud workloads for the solution.

611 Note: the first row in Table 4-1 does not contain information on the Cybersecurity Framework
612 subcategories and the NIST SP 800-53 Revision 4 controls that the public cloud hosting helps address.
613 That information is contained in the IBM Federal Cloud FedRAMP report. Since that report contains
614 sensitive information, it is not directly available. Organizations wanting access to that report would need
615 to have the necessary agreements in place with IBM first.

616 **Table 4-1 Products and Technologies Summary**

Component	Product	Version	Function	Cybersecurity Framework Subcategories	SP 800-53r4 Controls
Public Cloud Hosting	IBM Cloud and ICSV	Not applicable (N/A)	Provides IaaS capabilities for public cloud hosting at the FedRAMP moderate level.	Refer to the IBM Federal Cloud FedRAMP report.	Refer to the IBM Federal Cloud FedRAMP report.
Logging	vRLI	4.5.1	Provides real-time log management and log analysis with machine-learning-based intelligent grouping, high-performance searching, and troubleshooting across physical, virtual, and cloud environments.	PR.PT-1, DE.AE-1, DE.AE-2, DE.AE-3, DE.AE-4, DE.AE-5, DE.CM-1, DE.CM-7	AU-2, AU-3, AU-4, AU-5, AU-6, AU-7, AU-8, AU-9, AU-10, AU-11, AU-12
Operations Management	vROPS	6.6.1	Tracks and analyzes the operation of multiple data sources in the SDDC by using specialized analytic algorithms. These algorithms help vROPS learn and predict the behavior of every object that it monitors. Users access this information by views, reports, and dashboards.	PR.PT-1	AU-2, AU-6, AU-7, AU-8, AU-9
Cloud Management	vRB	7.3.1	Automates tracking and managing cloud costing, and resource consumption analysis and comparison.	N/A	N/A

Component	Product	Version	Function	Cybersecurity Framework Subcategories	SP 800-53r4 Controls
Cloud Management	vRA	7.3	Provides a secure web portal where authorized administrators, developers, and business users can request new IT services and manage specific cloud and IT resources, while ensuring compliance with business policies.	PR.AC-3, PR.MA-1	AC-17, AC-20, MA-2, MA-3, MA-4, MA-5, MA-6, SC-15
Cloud Management	vRO	7.3	Provides the capability to develop complex automation tasks, as well as access and launch workflows from the VMware vSphere client, various components of vRealize Suite, or other triggering mechanisms.	PR.MA-1	MA-2, MA-3, MA-4, MA-5, MA-6
Virtual Infrastructure Management	vSphere vCS	6.5u1	Provides a centralized and extensible platform for managing the virtual infrastructure (VMware vSphere environments).	PR.MA-1	MA-2, MA-3, MA-4, MA-5, MA-6
Virtual Infrastructure Management	vSphere Update Manager (VUM)	6.5u1	Provides centralized, automated patch and version management for VMware ESXi hosts, appliances, and VMs.	PR.IP-3, PR.IP-12	CM-3, CM-4, RA-3, RA-5, SI-2
Virtual Infrastructure Networking	NSX-V	6.4	Creates a network virtualization layer. All virtual networks are created on top of this layer, which is an abstraction between the physical and virtual networks.	PR.AC-5, PR.PT-4	AC-4, SC-7
Virtual Infrastructure Storage	vSAN	6.6.1	Delivers flash-optimized, secure shared storage for virtualized workloads.	PR.DS-1, PR.DS-2	SC-8, SC-28

Component	Product	Version	Function	Cybersecurity Framework Subcategories	SP 800-53r4 Controls
Virtual Infrastructure Security	PSC	6.5u1	Controls infrastructure security functions, such as vCenter Single Sign-On, licensing, certificate management, and server reservation.	ID.AM-2, PR.AC-7, PR.DS-3, PR.MA-1	CM-8, IA-2, IA-3, IA-4, IA-5, MA-2, MA-3
Virtual Infrastructure Hypervisor	vSphere ESXi	6.5u1	Enterprise-class, type-1 hypervisor for deploying and servicing VMs.	PR.MA-1	MA-2, MA-3, MA-4
Virtual Infrastructure Data Synchronization	Site Recovery Manager (SRM)	6.5.1	A disaster recovery solution for vSphere VMs that automates the disaster recovery process and helps manage the synchronization of data between protected and recovery sites.	PR.IP-4, PR.IP-9	CP-9, CP-10
Virtual Infrastructure VM Replication	vR	6.5.1	A hypervisor-based, asynchronous replication solution for vSphere VMs.	N/A	N/A
Governance, Risk, and Compliance (GRC)	RSA Archer Suite	6.X	Governance and risk management workflow and dashboard.	PR.PT-1, DE.CM-1	AU-6, AU-7, CA-7, CM-3, SI-4
Logging	RSA NetWitness Suite	11.x	Compliance reporting.	PR.PT-1	AU-6, AU-7
Authentication	RSA SecurID Suite	N/A	Strong authentication for administrative access.	PR.AC-1, PR.AC-6, PR.AC-7	IA-2, IA-4, IA-5, IA-7
Networking Switch	Dell Networking S4048-ON Switch	OS9+	Leaf and spine switches for network architecture.	N/A	N/A

Component	Product	Version	Function	Cybersecurity Framework Subcategories	SP 800-53r4 Controls
Networking Switch	Dell Networking S3048-ON Switch	OS9+	In-band management network.	N/A	N/A
Storage Device	Dell EMC Unity	4.3.1	Unified storage solution.	N/A	N/A
Backup Solution	Data Domain Virtual Edition (DD VE)	4.0	Solution backup capabilities.	N/A	N/A
Compute	Dell PowerEdge Server	R730	Compute nodes for the solution.	N/A	N/A
Compute	Dell PowerEdge Server	R730	Compute nodes for the solution.	N/A	N/A
Physical Layer	Top-of-rack (TOR) Switches	N/A	Dell TOR switch.	N/A	N/A
Physical Layer	Traditional Storage	N/A	Unity Storage.	N/A	N/A
Business Continuity Layer	Backup	N/A	Avamar.	PR.IP-4	CP-9, CP-10
HSM – Network Attached	Gemalto SafeNet Luna Network HSM 6	FW 6.10.9 SW 6.2.2	Network-attached HSM root of trust for HTKC.	PR.AC-1, PR.DS-1, PR.DS-6	IA-5, IA-7, SA-18, SC-12, SC-13
HSM – Network Attached	Gemalto SafeNet Luna Network HSM 7	FW 7.0.1 SW 7.2.0-220	Network-attached HSM root of trust for Microsoft ADCS.	PR.AC-1, PR.DS-1, PR.DS-6	IA-5, IA-7, SA-18, SC-12, SC-13
HSM – USB Attached	Gemalto SafeNet Luna USB HSM	FW 6.10.9	USB HSM integrated with offline Microsoft Root CA.	PR.AC-1, PR.DS-1, PR.DS-6	IA-5, IA-7, SA-18, SC-12, SC-13

617 ## 4.3 NCCoE Cloud Solution Architecture

618 Figure 4-2 expands the high-level solution architecture first illustrated in Figure 4-1. The following
619 subsections provide additional details on the following parts of this architecture:

620   ▪ VMware cluster architectures (Section 4.3.1)

621   ▪ RSA cluster architecture (Section 4.3.2)

622   ▪ HSM architecture (Section 4.3.3)

623   ▪ HyTrust architecture (Section 4.3.4)

624   ▪ Dell leaf and spine switch architecture (Section 4.3.5)

625 **Figure 4-2 High-Level NCCoE Cloud Architecture**

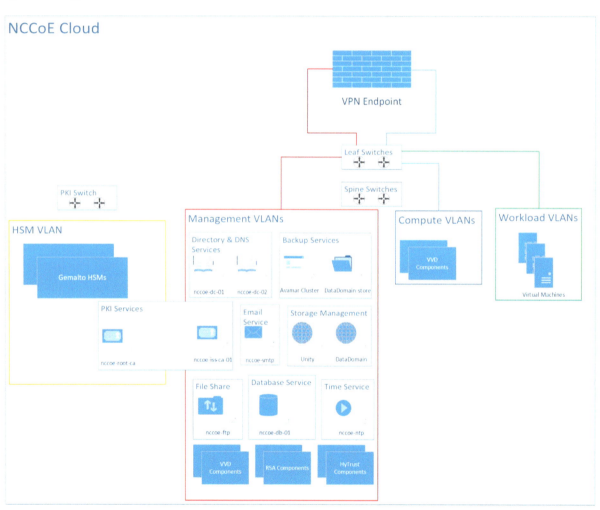

626

627   4.3.1   VMware Cluster Architectures

628   The diagrams of the VMware management cluster architecture (Figure 4-3) and compute cluster
629   architecture (Figure 4-4) are based on several assumptions about the data centers in which the VVD
630   would be implemented, including the following assumptions:

631   ▪   use of the leaf-spine architecture

632   ▪   use of Border Gateway Protocol (BGP) routing

633   ▪   availability of dedicated VLANs

634   ▪   ability to configure jumbo frames

635   ▪   Network File System (NFS) storage availability

636   ▪   use of vSAN Ready Nodes (optional)

637   ▪   availability of existing data-center services, such as Active Directory, DNS, SMTP, and NTP

638   The components described below are included in the VVD for an SDDC.

639   vSphere provides a powerful, flexible, and secure foundation for the SDDC. The vSphere solution
640   includes the vCS and the PSC to provide a centralized platform for managing the virtual infrastructure.
641   Within the VVD, PSC high availability is achieved by utilizing load balancers across multiple appliances.
642   Additionally, dedicated vCSs are deployed to manage clusters designated for infrastructure management
643   workloads and for compute or customer workloads. Optionally, VMware vSAN is defined within the VVD
644   to pool together storage devices across the vSphere cluster to create a distributed shared datastore.

645   The VVD includes VMware NSX to virtualize the network; this solution abstracts the network from the
646   underlying physical infrastructure. The VVD NSX solution ensures a highly available solution by utilizing
647   both equal-cost multi-path (ECMP)-enabled and high-availability-enabled appliances. ESGs configured to
648   utilize the BGP routing protocol are configured as ECMP pairs and act as the north-south boundary.
649   Routing within the logical space, east-west, is provided by high-availability-enabled distributed logical
650   routers. In this solution, VXLAN overlays the existing Layer 3 network infrastructure, addressing
651   scalability problems associated with cloud computing environments.

652   vRLI provides deep operational visibility and faster troubleshooting across physical, virtual, and cloud
653   environments. In this solution, vRLI is designed to provide a highly available solution for each site where
654   logs can be forwarded to a remote site for retention.

655   vROPS provides administrators with the ability to efficiently manage capacity and performance while
656   also gaining visibility across the virtual infrastructure. vROPS in the VVD is designed to provide high
657   availability while also ensuring that remote data centers are monitored. Within this design, in case of a
658   disaster, it is possible to failover the necessary vROPS components while leaving remote collectors at
659   their designated data centers.

660　vRA provides a portal where authorized individuals can request new IT services and manage cloud and IT
661　workloads. Requests for IT services, including infrastructure, applications, desktops, and many others,
662　are processed through a common service catalog to provide a consistent user experience despite the
663　underlying heterogenous infrastructure. In this design, the "Large" reference architecture for vRA is
664　followed, allowing for high availability and scalability up to 50,000 managed machines. The vRA solution
665　includes embedded VMware Identity Manager and embedded vRO.

666　vRB automates cloud cost management, consumption metering, and cloud comparison, delivering cost
667　visibility. vRB is integrated with vRA, providing cost information for the solution and pricing information
668　per blueprint. vRB is architected to include a remote collector at each site while the vRB appliance
669　remains in proximity to the vRA solution. vRB is protected by vSphere High Availability.

Figure 4-3 VMware Management Cluster Architecture

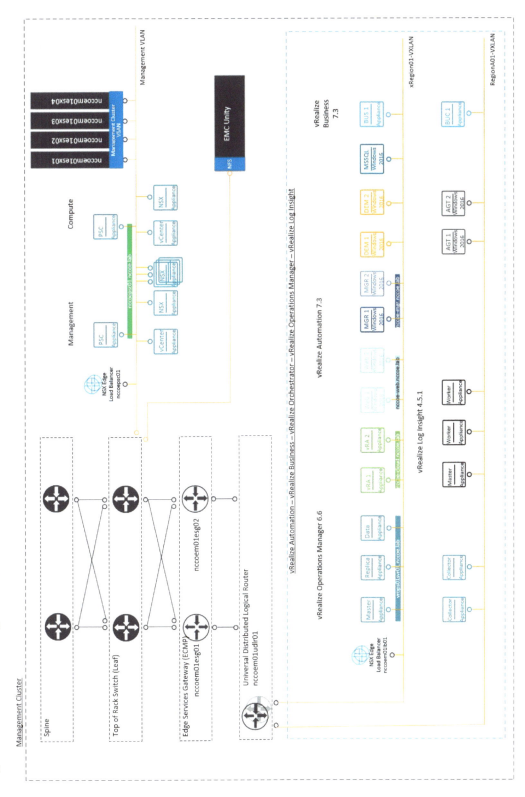

DRAFT

Figure 4-4 VMware Compute Cluster Architecture

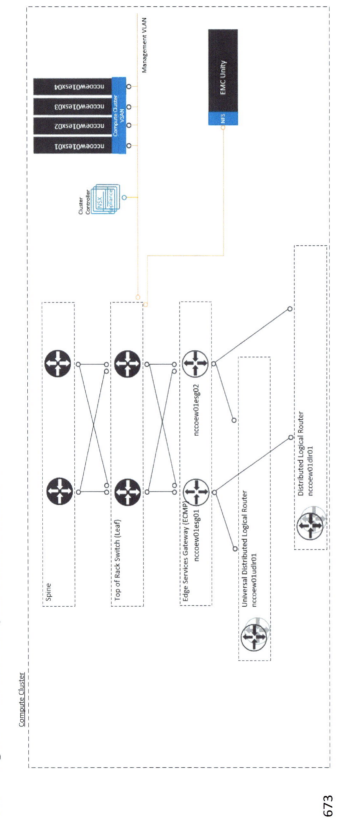

672

673

674   ## 4.3.2   RSA Cluster Architecture

675   [Figure 4-5](#) depicts the architecture of the RSA cluster. Within this cluster, the RSA SecurID Suite provides
676   strong authentication for administrator access to critical trusted cloud infrastructure components. RSA
677   NetWitness collects, analyzes, reports on, and stores log data from a variety of sources, to support
678   security policy and regulatory compliance requirements across the trusted cloud deployment. Finally,
679   the RSA Archer risk management solution instantiates compliance with applicable requirements, such as
680   FISMA, PCI DSS, and HIPAA, as well as industry-neutral voluntary frameworks like the NIST Cybersecurity
681   Framework, for this trusted cloud deployment.

682   **Figure 4-5 RSA Cluster**

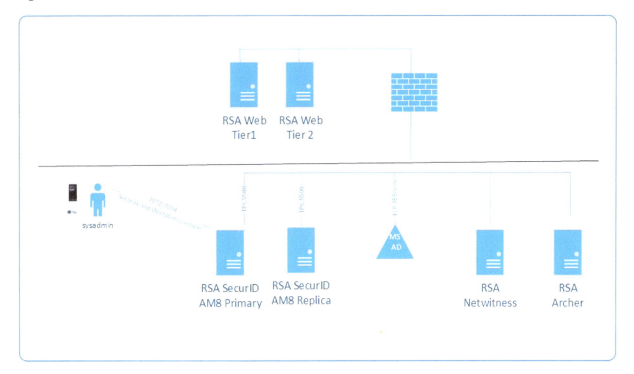

683

684   ## 4.3.3   HSM Architecture

685   [Figure 4-6](#) shows the HSM architecture in the NCCoE cloud. The following components are of the
686   greatest interest:

687   ▪   The SafeNet USB HSM is a small form-factor physical device connected via USB to the Microsoft
688   Root CA Server. To sign and issue a new Issuing CA certificate, the SafeNet USB HSM must be
689   connected directly to the Root CA. Because the SafeNet USB HSM is primarily used to protect
690   the Root CA's keys, it is typically stored securely in a vault. The SafeNet USB HSM is backed up
691   (i.e., cloned) to a secondary SafeNet USB HSM for redundancy.

692　　　▪　SafeNet Luna Network HSM 7 is a network-attached HSM that is tightly integrated with the
693　　　　　Microsoft Issuing CA that is located on a VM in the management cluster as a root of trust for
694　　　　　FIPS 140-2 Level 3 Compliance.

695　　　▪　SafeNet Luna Network HSM 6 is a network-attached HSM integrated with HTKC as a root of trust
696　　　　　for FIPS 140-2 Level 3 Compliance.

697　**Figure 4-6 HSM Architecture in the NCCoE Cloud**

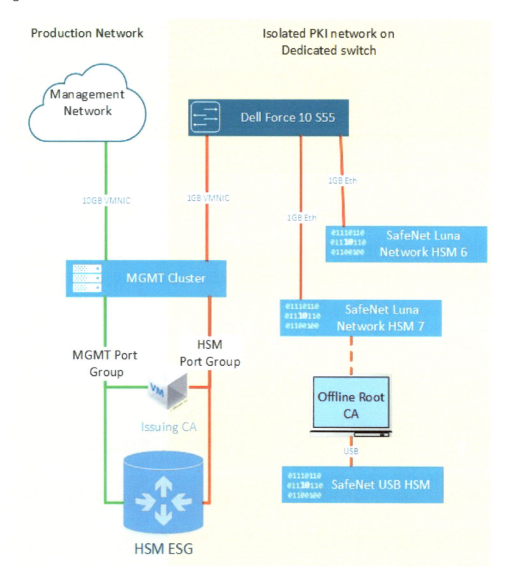

698

DRAFT

4.3.4 HyTrust Architecture

699

700 The NCCoE trusted cloud includes several HyTrust security components, including encryption and key
701 management, data discovery and classification, and advanced security for vSphere. From a placement
702 standpoint, the locations of the HyTrust appliances are shown in Figure 4-7.

703 **Figure 4-7 HyTrust Architecture in the NCCoE Cloud**

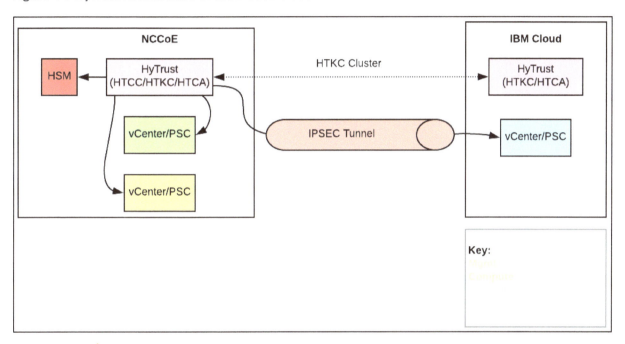

704

705 The following items explain where each type of HyTrust appliance is located within the architecture and
706 what functions it is providing:

707 ▪ HTCC provides advanced security features to vSphere. Additionally, HTCC Compliance is used to
708 verify the compliance of ESXi hosts. Users access vSphere via the "Published IP [Internet
709 Protocol]" (PIP) via the HTCC transparent proxy. Approved actions are passed through to
710 vSphere via a service account. Finally, HTCC conducts trust attestation for Intel TXT/TPM, to
711 provide hardware verification for HTBC. HTCC will be placed in the NCCoE management cluster.
712 HTCC will be configured with two virtual appliances in an active/passive cluster. That HTCC
713 cluster will service all three vSphere implementations.

714 ▪ HTKC provides key management to both HTDC in-guest encryption agents and vSANs for
715 storage-level encryption. HTKC leverages the NCCoE SafeNet Luna HSM for hardware
716 administration key storage. HTKC is configured as a trusted key management service in vCenter
717 to provide key management to vSAN. Two HTKC nodes will be placed in the NCCoE management
718 cluster, and two HTKC nodes will be placed in the IBM Cloud, with all four nodes in the same
719 fully active cluster. Figure 4-8 depicts this cluster.

720   ▪   HTCA will be placed in the NCCoE management cluster and the IBM Cloud. There will be one
721   HTCA node per location, and the nodes will not be clustered.

722   **Figure 4-8 HTKC Node Deployments**

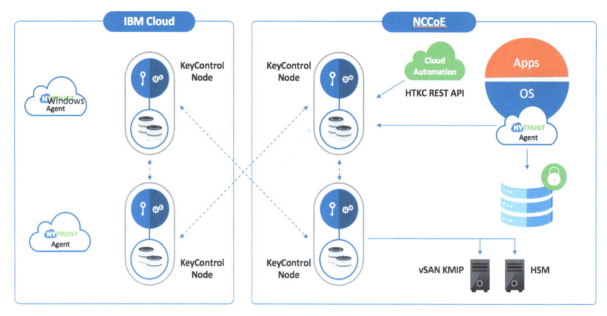

HyTrust KeyControl Active-Active Cluster

723

724   ## 4.3.5 Dell Leaf and Spine Switch Architecture

725   The core physical networking required for the components within the NCCoE cloud is comprised of four
726   Dell S4048-ON switches and two Dell S4048-ON switches, as shown in Figure 4-9. The Dell S4048-ON
727   switches are configured in a typical leaf-spine topology, with 40-gigabit (GB) interfaces for the
728   interconnections between the switches. The spine switches are in place to handle any east-west traffic
729   that may happen with the data center, while the leaf switches are in place to handle traffic for adjacent
730   servers, as well as northbound traffic out of the NCCoE Cloud.

731   All of the Dell PowerEdge R740xd servers that comprise the ESXi servers have redundant 10 GB links
732   connected to each of the leaf servers, for direct communication with each other. The leaf switches have
733   a Virtual Link Tunnel interconnect (VLTi) between them to provide Layer 2 aggregation between the two
734   switches. The BGP is also enabled on the leaf switches so that they can share routes with the spine
735   switches, and also allow the VMware NSX components to pair with them so that the leaf switches can
736   receive routing information from NSX. The two Dell S3048-ON switches are stacked together by 10 GB
737   interfaces so that they appear as one logical unit. The Dell S3048-ON switches also each use a 10 GB Link
738   Aggregate (LAG) connection as an uplink to the leaf switches. The uplink from the two Dell S3048-ON
739   switches to the leaf switches is necessary because the two Dell S3048-ON switches are mainly 1 GB

740 Ethernet ports supporting components in the environment that have only 1 GB Ethernet connections
741 and that need to communicate with devices that use 10 GB Enhanced Small Form-Factor Pluggable
742 (SFP+) connections.

743 **Figure 4-9 NCCoE Layer 3 Leaf – Spine Logical Network Diagram**

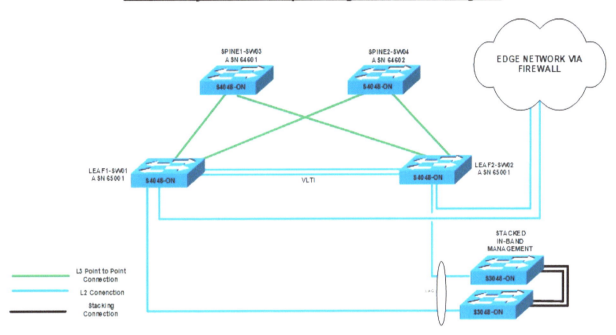

744

4.4 IBM Cloud Solution Architecture

746 ICSV is deployed on the IBM Cloud infrastructure according to a VMware, HyTrust, IBM, and Intel-
747 validated design reference architecture. The architecture depicted in Figure 4-10 is hosted on a
748 minimum of four bare-metal servers with Intel TXT enabled. VMware vCS is used for hypervisors with
749 VMware vSphere stack as a service. The VMware environment is built on top of bare-metal servers and
750 vSAN storage, and it includes the automatic deployment and configuration of an easy-to-manage logical
751 edge firewall that is powered by VMware NSX. This provides full native access to the entire VMware
752 stack, including the vSphere 6.5 Enterprise Plus edition; the NSX for Service Providers edition; and the
753 centralized platform for management, vCS. The solution, coupled with Windows Active Directory, HTCC,
754 and HTDC, provides a solid foundation to address security and compliance concerns. The entire
755 environment can be provisioned in a matter of hours, and the elastic bare-metal infrastructure can
756 rapidly scale out its compute capacity when needed.

757 See Section 4.3 for more information on the architecture of the solution components from VMware,
758 HyTrust, and others. Because some of the same components are used for both clouds to extend the

759 management plane across the infrastructure, details of those components are omitted from this section
760 to avoid duplication.

761 **Figure 4-10 IBM Cloud Architecture**

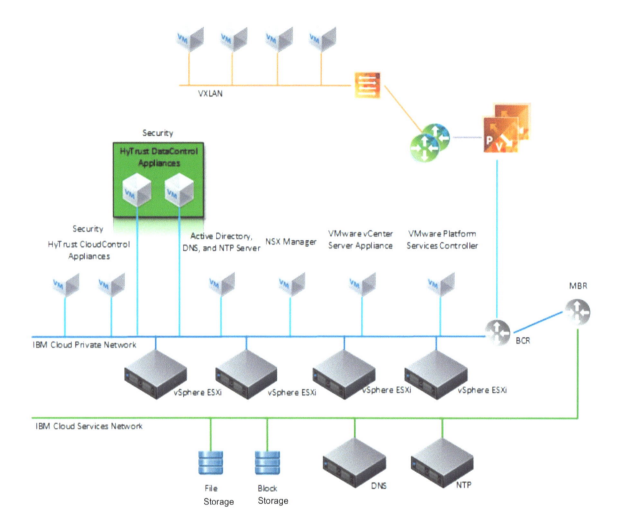

762

5 Security Characteristics Analysis

764 The purpose of the security characteristics analysis is to understand the extent to which the project
765 meets its objective of demonstrating a trusted cloud implementation leveraging commercial off-the-
766 shelf technology. In addition, it seeks to understand the security benefits and drawbacks of the example
767 solution.

768 **Because this is a preliminary draft, the security characteristics analysis for the example solution has**
769 **not yet been completed. The content provided in this section is preliminary and incomplete.**

770 5.1 Assumptions and Limitations

771 The security characteristics analysis will have the following limitations:

772 ▪ It is neither a comprehensive test of all security components nor a red-team exercise.

773 ▪ It cannot identify all weaknesses.

774 ▪ It does not include the lab infrastructure. It is assumed that devices are hardened. Testing these
775 devices would reveal only weaknesses in implementation that would not be relevant to those
776 adopting this reference architecture.

777 5.2 Demonstration of the Capabilities

778 The analysis will be based on defining a set of use case scenarios for the example solution, and then
779 demonstrating the security capabilities that can be achieved with the example solution for each use case
780 scenario. Each demonstration will be documented, including the basic steps performed and the security
781 capabilities achieved.

782 5.2.1 Use Case Scenario 1: Demonstrate Control and Visibility for the Trusted Hybrid
783 Cloud Environment

784 Assumptions for the trusted hybrid cloud environment (steps taken before the demonstrations occur)
785 are as follows:

786 1. The cryptographic, compute, storage, and network hardware components are secured and
787 hardened.

788 2. The VVD and the IBM Cloud for VMware – vCS have been instantiated on IBM Cloud stacks
789 through automation scripts.

790 3. The crypto network is separated and isolated from the management cluster and the tenant
791 workloads cluster.

792 4. The user accounts are isolated and secured based on defined functional roles following the
793 principle of least privilege.

794 5. The core components of the VVD and vCS, third-party software components, and all core
795 services are secured and hardened using recommended practices, such as vendor-developed or
796 community-developed secure configuration guides or DISA STIGs.

797 6. One or more industry-standard cloud service provider certifications, such as ISO, PCI, Cloud
798 Security Alliance (CSA), Service Organization Control (SOC), HIPAA, and FedRAMP, are leveraged.

799 Capability demonstrations:

1. Show the configuration of the hardware components, including the HSM, the compute node, the storage device, and the network switches.

800
801

2. Show the VVD and vCS stacks in vCenter (e.g., vSAN is encrypted).

802

3. Show the backup solution for the resiliency and recovery of workloads in a disaster-recovery scenario.

803
804

4. Show the three isolation domains, including the cryptographic, management, and tenant workloads in NSX.

805
806

5. Show multifactor authentication with an RSA SecurID token and the Active Directory domain groups and access rights structure.

807
808

6. Scan and show the secure configuration of VMware software components, such as ESXi, NSX, and Windows domain controller, by using CloudControl and a Windows configuration scanner. Figure 5-1 shows an example of results from a secure configuration scan.

809
810
811

812 **Figure 5-1 Example of Secure Configuration Scan Results**

Hosts	Host Type	Patch Level	Label	Last Run Template	Last Run	Compliance
10.121.71.133	ESXi Host	VMware ESXi 6.5.0 build-7967591	PII	N/A	Never	0%
10.121.71.135	ESXi Host			N/A	N/A	0%
192.168.4.105	VMware NSX	6.4.0.7564187		N/A	Never	0%
192.168.4.106	VMware NSX	6.4.0.7564187		N/A	Never	0%
cloud-vcenter.icsv.nccoe.lab	vCenter	6.5.0 build-6816762		N/A	N/A	
cloud-vcenter.icsv.nccoe.lab	vSphere Web Client Server			N/A	N/A	
comp-nccoe-esxi-01.nccoe.lab	ESXi Host	VMware ESXi 6.5.0 build-7388607		VMware 6.0 ESXi_Custom_Template	08/23/2018 12:14:24 PM	100%
comp-nccoe-esxi-02.nccoe.lab	ESXi Host	VMware ESXi 6.5.0 build-7388607	TRUSTED, PII	VMware 6.0 ESXi_Custom_Template	08/23/2018 12:14:24 PM	100%
comp-nccoe-esxi-03.nccoe.lab	ESXi Host	VMware ESXi 6.5.0 build-7388607	TRUSTED, PII	VMware 6.0 ESXi_Custom_Template	08/24/2018 10:25:14 AM	100%
comp-nccoe-esxi-04.nccoe.lab	ESXi Host	VMware ESXi 6.5.0 build-7388607	TRUSTED, PII	VMware 6.0 ESXi_Custom_Template	08/23/2018 12:14:24 PM	100%

813

7. Scan and show any software vulnerabilities of an ESXi node and a Microsoft workload.

814

8. Show the IBM FedRAMP report.

815

5.2.2 Use Case Scenario 2: Demonstrate Control of Workloads and Data Security

816

817 Assumptions for the trusted hybrid cloud environment (steps taken before the demonstrations occur) are as follows:

818

1. Workloads are encrypted and are running on a trusted compute node with a specific asset tag (PCI or HIPAA) within a mixed cluster.

819
820

2. Secondary approval is enforced for highly sensitive systems and/or operations.

821

822   Capability demonstrations:

823   1. Show that the workload on the trusted compute node is decrypted, as it matches the trust and
824   asset tag policy. Figure 5-2 shows examples of nodes with their labels (e.g., TRUSTED, PII).
825   Figure 5-3 shows verification that a workload on one of the nodes has been decrypted.

826   **Figure 5-2 Examples of Trusted Compute Nodes**

827

828   **Figure 5-3 Example of Decrypted Workload**

829

830   2. Migrate the workload to a compute node without the same asset tag policy, and show that the
831   workload cannot be decrypted on the untrusted compute node. Figure 5-4 presents an example
832   of a workload running on a server that does not have any tags. Figure 5-5 shows that the same
833   workload cannot be decrypted because the server on which it runs lacks the necessary tags.

834   **Figure 5-4 Example of Workload on Untagged Server**

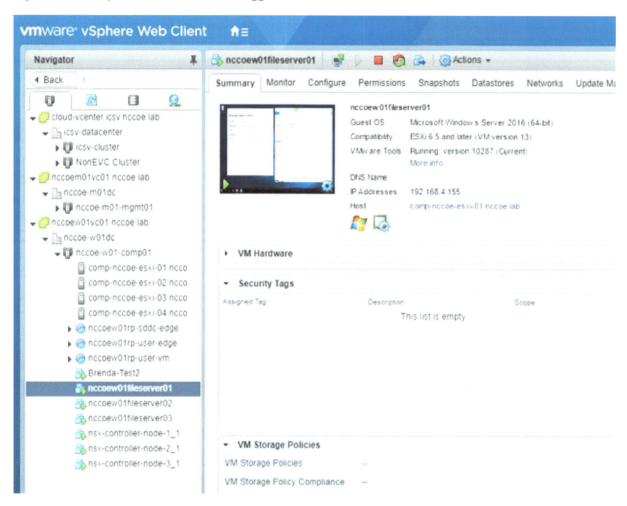

835

836   **Figure 5-5 Example of Workload that Cannot Be Decrypted**

837

838   3. Migrate the workload back to a trusted compute node, and show that the workload can be
839   decrypted and that the data can be accessed on the trusted compute node. <u>Figure 5-6</u> shows
840   that the workload has been migrated to a trusted and tagged server. <u>Figure 5-7</u> shows that the
841   workload can decrypt its data again because it is running on a trusted and tagged server.

842   **Figure 5-6 Example of Workload Migrated to Trusted and Tagged Server**

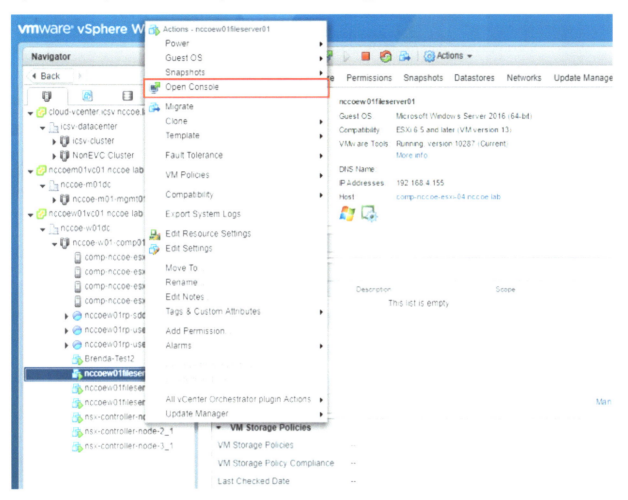

843

844   **Figure 5-7 Example of Workload Running on Trusted and Tagged Server**

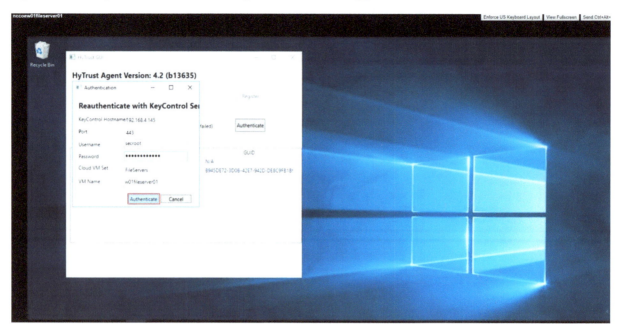

845

846   4. Show that two individuals are required to authorize the deletion of a high-value asset.

847   5. Scan and classify data based on a data classification schema, such as personally identifiable
848   information.

5.2.3 Use Case Scenario 3: Demonstrate a Workload Security Policy in a Hybrid
849
850   Cloud

851   Assumptions for the trusted hybrid cloud environment (steps taken before the demonstrations occur)
852   are as follows:

853   1. The trusted on-premises environment has been instantiated.

854   2. A secure connection has been established between the on-premises environment and the public
855   cloud instance.

856   3. The security capabilities from the on-premises environment have been extended to the public
857   cloud instance by integrating it into the on-premises management plane.

858   4. A three-tier web application is running in the on-premises environment with a specified security
859   policy (e.g., data protection, network segmentation, compliance requirements).

860   Capability demonstrations:

861   1.   Show that the three-tier web application's security policy is enforced within the on-premises
862   environment.

863   2.   Show that the three-tier web application can be migrated from the on-premises environment to
864   the public cloud instance.

865   3.   Show that the three-tier web application's security policy is persistent after the migration to the
866   public cloud instance.

867   5.3   Assessment Findings

868   After the demonstrations described in Section 5.2 have been performed, this section will assess how
869   well the solution addresses the security characteristics that it was intended to support. The findings will
870   be documented in terms of the NIST Cybersecurity Framework subcategories and NIST SP 800-53
871   Revision 4 controls identified in Appendix A, to help organize the results.

Appendix A   Mappings

873 The tables in this appendix include all the National Institute of Standards and Technology (NIST)
874 Cybersecurity Framework subcategories and NIST Special Publication (SP) 800-53 Revision 4 controls
875 listed in Section 4.2.8—those provided by individual components of the solution—and also list
876 additional subcategories and controls provided by the solution as a whole, not an individual component.

877 **Table A-1 List of NIST SP 800-53 Revision 4 Controls Addressed by Solution**

ID	Control Description
Access Control (AC)	
AC-3	Access Enforcement
AC-4	Information Flow Enforcement
AC-17	Remote Access
AC-20	Use of External Information Systems
Audit and Accountability (AU)	
AU-2	Audit Events
AU-3	Content of Audit Records
AU-4	Audit Storage Capacity
AU-5	Response to Audit Processing Failures
AU-6	Audit Review, Analysis, and Reporting
AU-7	Audit Reduction and Report Generation
AU-8	Time Stamps
AU-9	Protection of Audit Information
AU-10	Non-Repudiation
AU-11	Audit Record Retention
AU-12	Audit Generation
Security Assessment and Authorization (CA)	
CA-7	Continuous Monitoring
Configuration Management (CM)	
CM-3	Configuration Change Control
CM-4	Security Impact Analysis
CM-8	Information System Component Inventory

ID	Control Description
CM-9	Configuration Management Plan
CM-10	Software Usage Restrictions
Identification and Authentication (IA)	
IA-2	Identification and Authentication (Organizational Users)
IA-3	Device Identification and Authentication
IA-4	Identifier Management
IA-5	Authenticator Management
IA-7	Cryptographic Module Authentication
Maintenance (MA)	
MA-2	Controlled Maintenance
MA-3	Maintenance Tools
MA-4	Nonlocal Maintenance
MA-5	Maintenance Personnel
MA-6	Timely Maintenance
Risk Assessment (RA)	
RA-3	Risk Assessment
RA-5	Vulnerability Scanning
System and Services Acquisition (SA)	
SA-18	Tamper Resistance and Detection
System and Communications Protection (SC)	
SC-2	Application Partitioning
SC-3	Security Function Isolation
SC-7	Boundary Protection
SC-8	Transmission Confidentiality and Integrity
SC-12	Cryptographic Key Establishment and Management
SC-13	Cryptographic Protection
SC-15	Collaborative Computing Devices
SC-16	Transmission of Security Attributes
SC-28	Protection of Information at Rest

ID	Control Description
System and Information Integrity (SI)	
SI-2	Flaw Remediation
SI-4	Information System Monitoring
SI-7	Software, Firmware, and Information Integrity

878   **Table A-2 List of NIST Cybersecurity Framework Subcategories Addressed by Solution**

Cybersecurity Framework Subcategory Identifier	Cybersecurity Framework Subcategory Name
Identify (ID)	
ID.AM-2	Software platforms and applications within the organization are inventoried.
Protect (PR)	
PR.AC-1	Identities and credentials are issued, managed, verified, revoked, and audited for authorized devices, users and processes.
PR.AC-3	Remote access is managed.
PR.AC-5	Network integrity is protected (e.g., network segregation, network segmentation).
PR.AC-6	Identities are proofed and bound to credentials and asserted in interactions.
PR.AC-7	Users, devices, and other assets are authenticated (e.g., single-factor, multifactor) commensurate with the risk of the privacy risks and other organizational risks).
PR.DS-1	Data-at-rest is protected.
PR.DS-2	Data-in-transit is protected.
PR.DS-3	Assets are formally managed throughout removal, transfers, and disposition.
PR.DS-6	Integrity checking mechanisms are used to verify software, firmware, and information integrity.
PR.IP-3	Configuration change control processes are in place.
PR.IP-4	Backups of information are conducted, maintained, and tested.
PR.IP-9	Response plans (Incident Response and Business Continuity) and recovery plans (Incident Recovery and Disaster Recovery) are in place and managed.
PR.IP-12	A vulnerability management plan is developed and implemented.

Cyber-security Frame-work Sub-category Identifier	Cybersecurity Framework Subcategory Name
PR.MA-1	Maintenance and repair of organizational assets are performed and logged, with approved and controlled tools.
PR.PT-1	Audit/log records are determined, documented, implemented, and reviewed in accordance with policy.
PR.PT-4	Communications and control networks are protected.
Detect (DE)	
DE.AE-1	A baseline of network operations and expected data flows for users and systems is established and managed.
DE.AE-2	Detected events are analyzed to understand attack targets and methods.
DE.AE-3	Event data are collected and correlated from multiple sources and sensors.
DE.AE-4	Impact of events is determined.
DE.AE-5	Incident alert thresholds are established.
DE.CM-1	The network is monitored to detect potential cybersecurity events.
DE.CM-7	Monitoring for unauthorized personnel, connections, devices, and software is performed.

Appendix B   List of Acronyms

ACL	Access Control List
ADCS	Active Directory Certificate Services
BGP	Border Gateway Protocol
BIOS	Basic Input/Output System
CA	Certificate Authority
CloudSPF	Cloud Security Policy Framework
COSO	Committee of Sponsoring Organizations of the Treadway Commission
CRADA	Cooperative Research and Development Agreement
CSA	Cloud Security Alliance
DCG	Data Center Group
DD VE	Data Domain Virtual Edition
DFW	Distributed Firewall
DHCP	Dynamic Host Configuration Protocol
DISA	Defense Information Systems Agency
DLR	Distributed Logical Router
DNS	Domain Name System
ECMP	Equal-Cost Multi-Path
ESG	Edge Services Gateway
FAIR	Factor Analysis of Information Risk
FedRAMP	Federal Risk and Authorization Management Program
FIPS	Federal Information Processing Standard
FISMA	Federal Information Security Modernization Act
FOIA	Freedom of Information Act
GB	Gigabyte/Gigabit
GKH	Good Known Host

GRC	Governance, Risk, and Compliance
HIPAA	Health Insurance Portability and Accountability Act
HSM	Hardware Security Module
HTBC	HyTrust BoundaryControl
HTCA	HyTrust CloudAdvisor
HTCC	HyTrust CloudControl
HTDC	HyTrust DataControl
HTKC	HyTrust KeyControl
I/O	Input/Output
IaaS	Infrastructure as a Service
ICSV	IBM Cloud Secure Virtualization
IEEE	Institute of Electrical and Electronics Engineers
Intel AES-NI	Intel Advanced Encryption Standard – New Instructions
Intel CIT	Intel Cloud Integrity Technology
Intel TPM	Intel Trusted Platform Module
Intel TXT	Intel Trusted Execution Technology
Intel VT	Intel Virtualization Technology
IPsec	Internet Protocol Security
ISO	International Organization for Standardization
IT	Information Technology
KMIP	Key Management Interoperability Protocol
LAG	Link Aggregate
MLE	Measured Launch Environment
N/A	Not Applicable
NCCoE	National Cybersecurity Center of Excellence
NFS	Network File System

NIST	National Institute of Standards and Technology
NISTIR	National Institute of Standards and Technology Interagency Report
NSX-V	NSX for vSphere
NTP	Network Time Protocol
OS	Operating System
PC	Personal Computer
PCI DSS	Payment Card Industry Data Security Standard
PIP	Published Internet Protocol
PSC	Platform Services Controller
RMF	Risk Management Framework
SDDC	Software-Defined Data Center
SFP+	Enhanced Small Form-Factor Pluggable
SIEM	Security Information and Event Management
SMTP	Simple Mail Transfer Protocol
SNMP	Simple Network Management Protocol
SOC	Service Organization Control
SP	Special Publication
SRM	Site Recovery Manager
SSL	Secure Sockets Layer
STIG	Security Technical Implementation Guide
TLS	Transport Layer Security
TOR	Top-of-Rack
U.S.	United States
UDLR	Universal Distributed Logical Router
UDP	User Datagram Protocol
USB	Universal Serial Bus

DRAFT

vCS	vCenter Server
VDS	vSphere Distributed Switch
VIB	vSphere Installation Bundle
VLAN	Virtual Local Area Network
VLTi	Virtual Link Tunnel Interconnect
VM	Virtual Machine
VMM	Virtual Machine Manager
VMX	Virtual Machine Extensions
VPN	Virtual Private Network
vR	vSphere Replication
vRA	vRealize Automation
vRB	vRealize Business for Cloud
vRLI	vRealize Log Insight
vRO	vRealize Orchestrator
vROPS	vRealize Operations Manager
VTEP	VXLAN Tunnel Endpoint
VUM	vSphere Update Manager
VVD	VMware Validated Design
VXLAN	Virtual Extensible Local Area Network

Appendix C   Glossary

880

881 All significant technical terms used within this document are defined in other key documents,
882 particularly National Institute of Standards and Technology Interagency Report (NISTIR) 7904, *Trusted*
883 *Geolocation in the Cloud: Proof of Concept Implementation* [1]. As a convenience to the reader, terms
884 critical to understanding this volume are provided in this glossary.

Attestation	The process of providing a digital signature for a set of measurements securely stored in hardware, and then having the requester validate the signature and the set of measurements.
Cloud workload	A logical bundle of software and data that is present in, and processed by, a cloud computing technology.
Geolocation	Determining the approximate physical location of an object, such as a cloud computing server.
Hardware root of trust	An inherently trusted combination of hardware and firmware that maintains the integrity of information.
Trusted compute pool	A physical or logical grouping of computing hardware in a data center that is tagged with specific and varying security policies. Within a trusted compute pool, the access and execution of applications and workloads are monitored, controlled, audited, etc. Also known as a *trusted pool*.

Appendix D   References

[1]   M. Bartock et al., "Trusted geolocation in the cloud: Proof of concept implementation," NIST, Gaithersburg, MD, NISTIR 7904, Dec. 2015. Available: https://doi.org/10.6028/NIST.IR.7904.

[2]   NIST, "National Cybersecurity Center of Excellence (NCCoE) trusted geolocation in the cloud building block," *Federal Register*, vol. 82, no. 90, pp. 21979-21980, May 11, 2017. Available: https://www.gpo.gov/fdsys/pkg/FR-2017-05-11/pdf/2017-09502.pdf.

[3]   Joint Task Force Transformation Initiative, "Guide for conducting risk assessments," NIST, Gaithersburg, MD, NIST SP 800-30 Revision 1, Sep. 2012. Available: https://doi.org/10.6028/NIST.SP.800-30r1.

[4]   Joint Task Force Transformation Initiative, "Guide for applying the risk management framework to federal information systems: A security life cycle approach," NIST, Gaithersburg, MD, NIST SP 800-37 Revision 1, Feb. 2010. Available: https://doi.org/10.6028/NIST.SP.800-37r1.

[5]   *Risk management – Guidelines*, ISO Standard 31000:2018, Feb. 2018. Available: https://www.iso.org/iso-31000-risk-management.html.

[6]   COSO, "Enterprise risk management – Integrating with strategy and performance," COSO, Jun. 2017. Available: https://www.coso.org/Pages/erm.aspx.

[7]   J. Freund and J. Jones, *Measuring and Managing Information Risk: A FAIR Approach*. Oxford, England: Butterworth-Heinemann, 2014.

[8]   NIST, "Framework for improving critical infrastructure cybersecurity," NIST, Gaithersburg, MD, Apr. 16, 2018, Version 1.1. Available: https://doi.org/10.6028/NIST.CSWP.04162018.

[9]   Joint Task Force Transformation Initiative, "Security and privacy controls for federal information systems and organizations," NIST, Gaithersburg, MD, NIST SP 800-53 Revision 4, Apr. 2013. Available: https://dx.doi.org/10.6028/NIST.SP.800-53r4.

[10]   VMware, "Architecture and design: VMware validated design for management and workload consolidation 4.2," VMware, Palo Alto, CA, Mar. 27, 2018. Available: https://docs.vmware.com/en/VMware-Validated-Design/4.2/vmware-validated-design-42-sddc-consolidated-architecture-design.pdf.

[11]   VMware, "Deployment for region A: VMware validated design for software-defined data center 4.2," VMware, Palo Alto, CA, Feb. 13, 2018. Available: https://docs.vmware.com/en/VMware-Validated-Design/4.2/vmware-validated-design-42-sddc-regiona-deployment.pdf.

915 [12] VMware, "Operational verification: VMware validated design for software-defined data center
916   4.2," VMware, Palo Alto, CA, Mar.27, 2018. Available: https://docs.vmware.com/en/VMware-
917   Validated-Design/4.2/vmware-validated-design-42-sddc-operational-verification.pdf.

918 [13] VMware, "Planning and preparation: VMware validated design for software-defined data center
919   4.2," VMware, Palo Alto, CA, Feb. 13, 2018. Available: https://docs.vmware.com/en/VMware-
920   Validated-Design/4.2/vmware-validated-design-42-sddc-planning-preparation.pdf.

www.ingramcontent.com/pod-product-compliance
Lightning Source LLC
Chambersburg PA
CBHW050935060326
40690CB00039B/501